Contents

1 Introducing Elements

Photoshop Elements
is a digital image-
editing program that
comprehensively spans the
gap between very basic
programs and professional-
level ones. This chapter
introduces the various
workspaces and modes of
Elements, shows how to
access them, and details what
can be done with each one.

Photoshop Elements can be bought online directly from Adobe, as well as from other computer and software sites, or at computer software stores. There are Windows and Mac versions of the program, and with Elements 2019 these are virtually identical. If Elements 2019 is bought from the Adobe website, at **www.adobe.com**, it can be downloaded and installed directly from there. Otherwise it will be provided on a CD, with a serial number that needs to be entered during installation.

The New icon pictured above indicates a new or enhanced feature introduced with the latest version – Photoshop Elements 2019 (also referred to as Elements 2019).

About Elements

Photoshop Elements is the offspring of the professional-level image-editing program, Photoshop. Photoshop is somewhat unusual in the world of computer software, in that it is widely accepted as being the best program of its type on the market. If professional designers or photographers are using an image-editing program, it will almost certainly be Photoshop. However, two of the potential drawbacks to Photoshop are its cost and its complexity. This is where Elements comes into its own. Adobe (the maker of Photoshop and Elements) has recognized that the majority of digital image users (i.e. the consumer market) want something with the basic power of Photoshop, but with enough user-friendly features to make it easy to use, and for a reasonable price. With the explosion in the digital camera and smartphone market, a product was needed to meet the needs of a new generation of image editors – that product is Photoshop Elements.

Elements contains most of the same powerful editing/color management tools as the full version of Photoshop, and it also includes a number of versatile features for sharing images and for creating artistic projects such as slideshows, cards, calendars and memes for sharing on social media. It also has valuable features, such as the Guided edit and Quick edit modes, where you can quickly apply editing techniques and follow step-by-step processes to achieve a range of creative and artistic effects.

Special effects
One of the great things about using Elements with digital images is that it provides numerous fun and creative options for turning mediocre images into eye-catching works of art. This is achieved

through a wide variety of step-by-step activities within Guided edit mode, which have been added to and enhanced in Elements 2019.

Advanced features
In addition to user-friendly features, Elements also has an Expert edit mode where you can use a range of advanced features, including a full set of tools for editing and color adjustments.

Home Screen

When you first open Elements, you will be presented with the Home Screen. This offers initial advice about working with Elements and also provides options for accessing the different workspaces. The Home Screen appears by default when Elements 2019 is opened, and it can also be accessed from the Home Screen button on the bottom Taskbar of either of the Elements modes, the Editor and the Organizer.

Home Screen functions

The Home Screen has a range of options covering tips about using Elements 2019 and also for accessing the different modes.

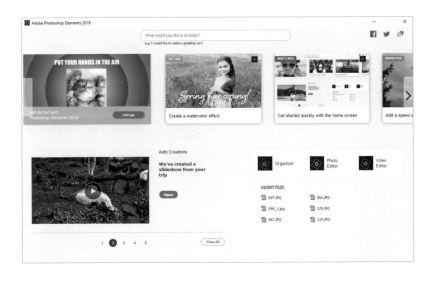

1. Click on the **Organizer** button to go to the section for organizing and managing photos

2. Click on the **Photo Editor** button to the section for editing and enhancing photos

3. Click on the **Video Editor** button to open Premiere Elements for working with video (if using Premiere Elements)

The Home Screen has been extensively revised in Elements 2019.

The Home Screen can also be accessed at any time by selecting **Help** > **Home Screen** from the Photo Editor or Organizer Menu bar.

Premiere Elements is the companion program for editing digital video. It can be bought separately, or in a two-program bundle with Photoshop Elements.

...cont'd

4 Click on this panel to access the Photoshop Elements 2019 help pages, detailing the latest features

5 The top panels can be used to get information about a range of creative photo techniques, such as slideshows and information about using the Home Screen

If a panel has a **Try This** tag on it, click on the **Try** button to go to the relevant section of Elements 2019, from where the selected action can be performed. If a panel has a **What's New** tag on it, click on the **Open Link** button to go to a help page with details about the item. These buttons appear when you move the cursor over the image.

Create a Slideshow

Get started quickly with the home screen

6 Click on the arrow at the right-hand side of the top panel to view more help options within the Home Screen for creating engaging photo projects

There are over three dozen options in the top panel of the Home Screen in Elements 2019.

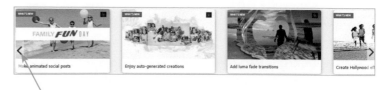

7 Click on the arrow at the left-hand side of the top panel to move back to the previous screen

8 One of the features of Elements 2019 is the ability to make Auto Creations. These are artistic slideshows and collages that are automatically created from groups of similar photos. On the Home Screen, Auto Creations are displayed in this panel

Auto Creations are a new feature in Elements 2019.

Click on the **Open** button to view an Auto Creation. Click on the **View All** button to see the full range of Auto Creations.

9 Click here to view the available Auto Creations

10 Below the Organizer, Photo Editor and Video Editor buttons, the most recently-opened files are displayed. Click on one to open it again in Elements 2019

For more information about Auto Creations, see pages 84-87.

11 Use the Search box at the top of the Home Screen to search for specific photographic techniques, such as changing the colors in a photo or creating a calendar

11

Photo Editor Workspace

From the Home Screen, the Photo Editor workspace can be accessed. This is a combination of the work area (where images are opened and edited), menus, toolbars, toolboxes and panels. At first it can seem a little daunting, but Elements has been designed with three different editing modes to give you as many options as possible for editing your photos.

The components of the Photo Editor (Editor) are:

Menu bar   Editor mode buttons   Panel bin

Toolbox   Taskbar   Work area

Editor modes

The three different modes in the Photo Editor are accessed from the buttons at the top of the Elements window. They are:

- **Quick edit mode**. This can be used to perform quick editing options in one step.

- **Guided edit mode**. This can be used to perform a range of editing techniques, following a step-by-step process for each.

- **Expert edit mode**. This can be used for ultimate control over the editing process.

12

The Elements Organizer can be accessed from any of the Editor modes by clicking on the Organizer button on the Taskbar.

The keyboard shortcut for closing Elements is Ctrl + Q (Command key + Q on a Mac).

...cont'd

Taskbar and Tool Options

The Taskbar is the group of buttons that is available across all three Editor modes, at the bottom left of the Elements window:

One of the options on the Taskbar is Tool Options. This displays the available options for any tool selected from the Toolbox (different tools are available in each of the different Editor modes). See pages 20-21 for details.

Photo Bin

The Photo Bin is another feature that can be accessed from all three Editor modes. The Photo Bin enables you to quickly access all of the images that you have open within the Editor. To use the Photo Bin:

 Open two or more images. The most recently-opened one will be the one that is active in the Editor window

 All open images are shown here in the Photo Bin

 Click on an image in the Photo Bin to make that the active one for editing

Don't forget

The items on the Taskbar are, from left to right: show or hide the Photo Bin, show or hide the Tool Options bar, Undo the previous actions, Redo any undone actions, Rotate the active photo, and access the Organizer. In Expert edit mode there is also an option to change the Layout.

Hot tip

Images can also be made active for editing by dragging them directly from the Photo Bin and dropping them within the Editor window.

Hot tip

When image editing has begun, this icon appears at its top right-hand corner in the Photo Bin.

13

Quick Edit Mode

Quick edit mode contains a number of functions that can be selected from panels and applied to an image, without the need to manually apply all of the commands. To do this:

For a more detailed look at Quick edit mode, see pages 88-91.

Some of the options in the Adjustments panel in Quick edit mode (Step 3) have an **Auto** option for applying the effect in a single click.

Move the cursor over one of the thumbnails to view a real-time preview of the effect on the open image. Click on one of the thumbnails to apply the effect.

1 In the Editor, click on the **Quick** button

2 The currently-active image is displayed within the Quick edit window. This has the standard Taskbar and Photo Bin, and a reduced Toolbox. Click here to access the Quick edit panels

3 Select one of the commands to have it applied to the active image. This can be applied either by clicking on one of the thumbnail options or by dragging the appropriate slider at the top of the panel

4 Click on these buttons on the Taskbar at the bottom of the Quick edit panel to select **Adjustments**, **Effects**, **Textures** and **Frames** options for adding to photos

Guided Edit Mode

Guided edit mode focuses on common tasks for editing digital images, and shows you how to perform them with a step-by-step process. To use Guided edit mode:

 1 In the Editor, click on the **Guided** button

 2 The Guided edit window contains a range of categories that can be accessed from buttons at the top of the window. Each category contains Guided edit options. Drag the mouse over each item to view the before and after effect

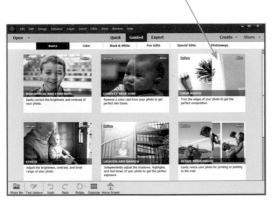

3 Each item has its own wizard to perform the required task. This will take you through a step-by-step process for undertaking the selected action. Move through the steps to complete the selected Guided edit option

Some new effects have been added to Guided edits in Elements 2019.

Guided edit mode is a great place to start if you are new to image editing, or feel unsure about anything to do with it.

Different Guided edits have varying numbers of steps in the required wizards, but the process is similar for all of them.

Expert Edit Mode

Expert edit mode is where you can take full editing control over your photos. It has a range of powerful editing tools so that you can produce subtle and impressive effects. To use Expert edit mode:

Select **Window** > **Tools** from the Menu bar to show or hide the Toolbox.

1 In the Editor, click on the **Expert** button

Expert

2 The full range of editing tools is available:

Expert edit mode Toolbox   Open panels

Tool Options button

When a tool is selected in the Toolbox, the Tool Options bar (above the Taskbar) has various options for the selected tool; see pages 20-21.

Taskbar Layout button   Expert edit mode panel buttons

The **Layout** button is the one addition on the Taskbar within Expert edit mode, as opposed to Quick and Guided edit modes. Click on the **Layout** button to access options for the display of your open photos within the Editor window.

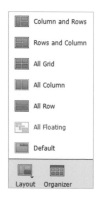

...cont'd

The Expert edit mode Toolbox

The Toolbox in Expert edit mode contains tools for applying a wide range of editing techniques. Some of the tools have more than one option. To see if a tool has additional options:

1 Move the cursor over the **Toolbox**. Tools that have additional options appear with a small arrow in the top right-hand corner of their icons. Click on a tool to view the options within the Tool Options bar

The default Toolbox tools are (keyboard shortcut in brackets):

Zoom (Z)	Hand (H)
Move (V)	Rectangular Marquee (M)
Lasso (L)	Quick Selection (A)
Eye (Y)	Spot Healing Brush (J)
Smart Brush (F)	Clone Stamp (S)
Blur (R)	Sponge (O)
Brush (B)	Eraser (E)
Paint Bucket (K)	Gradient (G)
Color Picker (I)	Custom Shape (U)
Type (T)	Pencil (N)
Crop (C)	Recompose (W)
Content-Aware (Q)	Straighten (K)
Foreground Color	Background Color

...cont'd

Panels

In Expert edit mode, Elements uses panels to group together similar editing functions and provide quick access to certain techniques. The panels can be accessed from the Window button on the Expert Menu bar and also from the respective buttons on the right-hand side of the Expert edit mode Taskbar. Click on the **More** button to access the full range of panels:

- **Actions**. This can be used to perform automated actions over a group of images at the same time.

- **Adjustments**. This can be used to add or make editing changes to adjustment layers in the Layers panel.

- **Color Swatches**. This is a panel for selecting colors that can then be applied to parts of an image, or elements that have been added to it.

- **Effects**. This contains special effects and styles that can be applied to an entire image or a selected part of an image. There are also filters that have their own dialog boxes, in which settings can be applied and adjusted. Layer Styles can also be applied to elements within an image.

- **Favorites**. This is where your favorite graphical elements from the Content panel can be stored and retrieved quickly.

- **Filters**. This can be used to add a range of filter effects to an image (see page 92 for details).

- **Graphics**. This contains graphical elements that can be added to images, including backgrounds, frame shapes and text.

- **Histogram**. This displays a graph of the tonal range of the colors in an image. It is useful for assessing the overall exposure of an image, and it changes as an image is edited.

- **History**. This can be used to undo any editing steps that have been performed. Every action is displayed and can be reversed by dragging the slider next to the most recent item.

Hot tip

The panels are opened in the Panel Bin, which is at the right of the Editor window. In Expert edit mode this can be collapsed or expanded by selecting **Window > Panel Bin** from the Menu bar.

Hot tip

Some panels can be opened directly with keyboard shortcuts. These are: Effects F6, Graphics F7, Info F8, Histogram F9, History F10, Layers F11 and Navigator F12.

Hot tip

Select **Window > Reset Panels** from the Menu bar to revert the panels to their original format. This is useful if you have been working with several panels and want to revert to the default.

- **Info**. This displays information about an image, or a selected element within it, including details about the color in an image or the position of a certain item.

- **Layers**. This enables several layers to be included within an image. This can be useful if you want to add elements to an existing image, such as shapes or text.

- **Navigator**. This can be used to move around an image and magnify certain areas of it.

- **Styles**. This can be used to add styles to the edge of an image, such as a bevel effect.

Working with panels

To work with panels in Expert edit mode:

1 Click on one of the panel buttons on the Taskbar on the previous page to open the related panel

2 If there are additional sections for a panel, click here to view the other options

3 Click on the **More** button to view the rest of the available panels

4 The additional panels are grouped together. Click on a tab to access the required panel. Click and drag on a tab to move the panel away from the rest of the group

Styles can only be applied to images that have been converted to layers (this can be done when the **Styles** button is selected).

Click here to access the menu for an open panel.

Do not have too many panels open at one time. If you do, the screen will become cluttered and it will be difficult to edit images effectively.

19

Tool Options Bar

When a tool is selected from the Toolbox, in either Expert or Quick mode, the Tool Options bar is activated on the Taskbar. This provides options for selecting different tools from that category (if there are any), and also settings for the currently selected tool. To use the Tool Options bar:

Don't forget

Use these buttons in the top right-hand corner of the Tool Options bar to, from left to right: access the Help options for the selected tool; access the Tool Options menu; or hide the Tool Options bar (click on a tool to display the Tool Options bar again).

 Select a tool from the Toolbox

 Click here on the Taskbar to hide or show the Tool Options bar

3 The Tool Options bar is positioned above the Taskbar at the bottom of the Elements window

Hot tip

Brush **Mode** has several options for how the brush stroke interacts with the background behind it; e.g. Color Burn, Lighten or Soft Light. These can be used to create artistic effects with the Brush tool and the photo itself.

4 Click here to select different tools from the selected category (in this example it is the Brush tool, the Impressionist Brush tool or the Color Replacement tool)

5 For each item there are different settings available; e.g. for the Brush tool there is **Brush** type, **Size** and **Opacity** (how much of the background is visible through the selected brush stroke). There are also options for a wider Brush range, including **Mode** and **Brush Settings...**

Don't forget

For a more detailed look at Brush style settings, see pages 162-163.

6 Other tools have different settings available from the Tool Options bar. For instance, the **Zoom** tool has options for zooming the currently active image to different magnifications, and also viewing it at specific sizes; e.g. **1:1**, **Fit Screen**, **Fill Screen** and **Print Size**

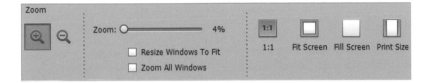

7 The **Type** tool has options for font type, font style, font color, font size, leading (the space between lines of text), bold, italics, underline, strikethrough and also text alignment (left, center or right)

The Type tool also has options for changing the orientation of text and also Text Warp for special effects; see page 150 for details.

8 For the **Marquee** tool and the **Lasso** tool there are options for editing a current selection (add to selection, subtract from selection and intersect with selection) and also for the amount of Feathering to be applied. This determines how much around the edge of the selection is slightly blurred, to give a soft-focus effect. The Marquee tool also has an option for setting a specific aspect for the selection; i.e. create it at a fixed ratio or size

The Marquee and Lasso tools are used to make selections by dragging the tool over the image. This can be symmetrical selections (e.g. Rectangular Marquee) or freehand (e.g. Lasso).

Menu Bar

In the Editor, the Menu bar contains menus that provide all of the functionality for the workings of Elements. Some of these functions can also be achieved through the use of the other components of Elements, such as the Toolbox, the Tool Options bar and the panels. However, the Menu bar is where all of the commands needed for the digital editing process can be accessed in one place.

Menu bar menus

- **File**. This has standard commands for opening, saving and printing images.

- **Edit**. This contains commands for undoing previous operations, and standard copy-and-paste techniques.

- **Image**. This contains commands for altering the size, shape and position of an image. It also contains more advanced functions such as changing the color mode of an image.

- **Enhance**. This contains commands for editing the color elements of an image. It also contains quick-fix options and commands for creating Photomerge effects such as panoramas and combining exposures.

- **Layer**. This contains commands for working with different layers within an image.

- **Select**. This contains commands for working with areas that have been selected within an image, with one of the selection tools in the Toolbox.

- **Filter**. This contains numerous filters that can be used to apply special effects to an image.

- **View**. This contains commands for changing the size at which an image is displayed, and also options for showing or hiding rulers and grid lines.

- **Window**. This contains commands for changing the way multiple images are displayed, and also options for displaying the components of Elements.

- **Help**. This contains the various Help options.

Although the Menu bar menus are all available in each of the Editor modes, some of the menu options are not available in Quick edit or Guided edit mode.

Elements does not support the CMYK color model for editing digital images. This could be an issue if you use a commercial printer.

22

The Mac version of Elements also has a Photoshop Elements menu on the Menu bar. This contains the Preferences options (see next page).

Preferences

A number of preferences can be set within Elements to determine the way the program operates. It is perfectly acceptable to leave all of the default settings as they are, but as you become more familiar with the program you may want to change some of the preference settings. Preferences can be accessed by selecting **Edit** > **Preferences** from the Menu bar (**Adobe Photoshop Elements Editor** > **Preferences** in the Mac version). The available ones are:

- **General**. This contains a variety of options for selecting items, such as shortcut keys.

- **Saving Files**. This determines the way Elements saves files.

- **Performance**. This determines how Elements allocates memory when processing editing tasks.

- **Scratch Disks**. This determines how Elements allocates disk space when processing editing tasks (referred to as "scratch disks"). If you require more memory for editing you can do this by allocating up to four scratch disks. These act as extra areas from which memory can be used during editing.

- **Display & Cursors**. This determines how cursors operate when certain tools are selected.

- **Transparency**. This determines the color or transparency of the background on which an open image resides.

- **Units & Rulers**. This determines the unit of measurement used by items such as rulers.

- **Guides & Grids**. This determines the color and format of any guides and grids that are used.

- **Plug-Ins**. This displays any plug-ins that have been downloaded to enhance image editing with Elements.

- **Adobe Partner Services** and **Update Options**. These can be used to check for related services and determine how updates to Elements are delivered.

- **Type**. This determines how text appears on images.

- **Country/Region Selection**. This is used to select the location from where you are using Elements.

Each preference has its own dialog box, in which the specific preference settings can be made.

A scratch disk is an area of temporary storage on the hard drive that can be utilized if the available memory (RAM) has been used up.

Guides and grids can be accessed from the View menu in Editor mode.

Organizer Workspace

The Organizer workspace contains functions for sorting, viewing and finding multiple images. To use the Organizer:

Organizer mode can be used with touchscreen devices by pressing on the screen.

 In any of the Editor modes, click on the **Organizer** button on the Taskbar

The Organizer has four views, accessed from these buttons:

- Media View **Media**
- People View **People**
- Places View **Places**
- Events View **Events**

Images displayed in the Media View can be located from anywhere on your computer. The thumbnails in Media View are just references to the originals, wherever they are stored.

Media View

The Media View displays thumbnails of your photos, and also has functions for sorting and finding images:

Folders and Albums   View buttons   Thumbnails

Photos can be selected within the Organizer, and then opened in an Editor mode by clicking on this button on the Organizer Taskbar.

Organizer Taskbar   Tag/Info button

24

...cont'd

1 Click on these buttons to apply image-editing effects to a selected image in Media View, or view the Tags and Information panels

For information about using tags and keywords, see pages 48-49.

People View
This view can be used to tag specific people and then view photos with those people in them.

For information about using the Organizer, and its different views, see Chapter 2.

Places View
This view can be used to place photos on a map so that they can be searched for by location.

When you have a group of photos from the same location, add them to Places View so that this can be used to search over your photos.

Events View
This view can be used to group photos according to specific events such as birthdays and vacations.

25

Create Mode

Create mode is where you can release your artistic flair and start designing items such as photo books and photo collages. It can also be used to create slideshows, and to put your images onto discs. To use Create mode:

Use your 12 best photos when using the Photo Calendar option.

Beware

Create mode projects take longer than normal image-editing functions.

 In either the Editor or the Organizer, click on the **Create** button

Create ▾

 Select one of the Create projects. Each project has a wizard that takes you through the Create process. The projects include Photo Books, Greeting Cards, Photo Calendars, Photo Collages, and covers for CDs/ DVDs

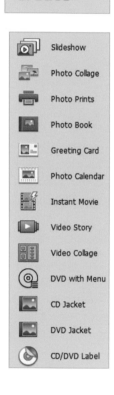

Slideshow
Photo Collage
Photo Prints
Photo Book
Greeting Card
Photo Calendar
Instant Movie
Video Story
Video Collage
DVD with Menu
CD Jacket
DVD Jacket
CD/DVD Label

The Create wizard takes you through the process so you can display your photos in a variety of creative ways

For most creations there is a theme that can be applied, to which your own photos can then be added

Click on the **Print** button once a creation has been made, to produce a hard copy.

 Your photos can be added automatically from the Photo Bin, or you can drag them directly from there onto the creation

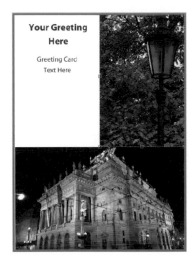

Your Greeting Here

Greeting Card Text Here

Once your photos have been added, a new file is created, to which you can add text, layout designs and graphics. Click on any available text boxes to add text there, click on the **Layouts** button to change the layout of the creation, and click on the **Graphics** button to add a background

Click on the **Save** button to save a completed creation in a specific file format, and the **Close** button to exit Create mode without saving the project.

Click on the **Advanced Mode** button to access the Expert mode Toolbox, which can be used to edit the creation in the same way as for a standard photo

Advanced Mode

Share Mode

Share mode can be used to distribute your images to family and friends in a number of creative ways. To use Share mode:

The Share function can also be accessed from within the Editor, but there are fewer share options available.

 1 In the Organizer, click on the **Share** button

Share ▾

2 Select one of the Share options, such as sharing to social media sites, sharing via email or creating a DVD or PDF slideshow

To share an image in an email you need to have an appropriate email app on your computer, and an internet connection.

3 If you are sharing to email, the selected item is added to a wizard that can be used to determine the size and quality of the attachment that you want to send. Click on the **Next** button to move through the wizard

4 For sharing to social media sites such as Flickr and Twitter, Elements has to initially be authorized to share content to these sites. Click on the **Authorize** button to give Elements permission to share to the selected app

There is always some risk in giving websites authorization to access your computer.

5 Enter your login details for the selected site and click on the **Authorise app** button (note that the spellings are localized)

6 In the Elements window, click on the **Done** button to give Elements permission to share with the selected app

You must already have an account with a specific social media site in order to authorize Elements to use it; you cannot create an account during this process.

7 Once permission has been given for a social media site, you can share photos to the site by clicking on the **Share** button at the top of the Elements window, selecting the required app and entering the necessary information; i.e. a caption

You only have to authorize Elements to use a social media site once. After that, photos can be shared in two clicks from the **Share** menu.

29

Getting Help

One of the differences between Elements and the full version of Photoshop is the amount of assistance and guidance offered by each program. Since Photoshop is aimed more at the professional end of the market, the level of help is confined largely to the standard help directory, which serves as an online manual. Elements also contains this, but in addition it has the Getting Started option, which is designed to take users through the digital image-editing process as smoothly as possible. The Getting Started option offers general guidance about digital imaging techniques and there are also help items that can be accessed by selecting Help from the Menu bar. These include online help; information on available plug-ins for Elements; tutorials; and support details.

Using the help files

 Select **Photoshop Elements Help** from the **Help** menu and click on an item to display it in the main window. Click on the links at the left-hand side to navigate through each section

Hot tip

A range of help options can also be accessed from the Home Screen.

Hot tip

The keyboard shortcut for Photoshop Elements Help is F1.

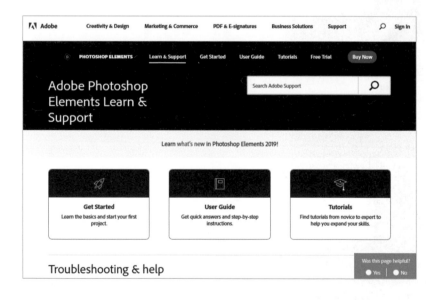

2 Organizing Images

This chapter shows how to download digital images via Elements and how to view and organize them, including using the People, Places, and Events views. It shows how you can tag images so that they are easy to find, how to search for items according to a variety of criteria, and how to use albums and folders to organize and manage images in the Organizer.

Obtaining Images

One of the first tasks in Elements is to import images so that you can start editing and sharing them. This can be done from a variety of devices, but the process is similar for all of them. To import images into Elements:

Don't forget

For many digital cameras, the Photo Downloader window will appear automatically once the camera is connected to the computer. However, if this does not happen it will have to be accessed manually as shown here.

 Access the **Organizer** by clicking on this button in the Editor

Organizer

 Select **File** > **Get Photos and Videos** from the Menu bar and select the type of device from which you want to load images into Elements, or

From Files and Folders...	Ctrl+Shift+G
From Camera or Card Reader...	Ctrl+G
From Scanner...	Ctrl+U
In Bulk...	

Hot tip

The keyboard shortcut for obtaining images from a camera or card reader is Ctrl + G (Command key + G on a Mac).

 Click on the **Import** button and select one of the options for obtaining images

Import ▾

From Files and Folders...

From Camera or Card Reader...

From Scanner...

In Bulk...

Hot tip

Images can also be imported from existing files and folders on your computer. After this has been done, they will be added to the Organizer's database and you will be able to apply all of its features to the images.

4 If you select **From Camera or Card Reader...**, click the drop-down arrow beside **Get Photos from:** to select a specific device. This can include directly from a digital camera (connected to your computer with a USB cable), a smartphone or a memory card, using a memory card reader

Get Photos from:

Apple iPhone	∨
Apple iPhone	
E:\<Camera or Card Reader>	
< Refresh List >	

5 The number of files selected to be downloaded are shown under the **Get Photos from:** drop-down box in the Photo Downloader window

6 Click the **Browse...** button to select a destination for the selected images

Elements Organizer - Photo Downloader ✕

Source

Get Photos from:

E:\<Camera or Card Reader> ∨

1293 Files Selected - 7.3GB (295 Duplicates Excluded)

Import Settings

Location: C:\Users\Nick\Pictures\[Shot Date] [Browse...]

Create Subfolder(s): Shot Date (yyyy mm dd) ∨

Rename Files: Do not rename files ∨
＿＿＿＿＿ + ＿
Example: DSC_0586.JPG
☐ Preserve Current Filename in XMP

Delete Options: After Copying, Do Not Delete Originals ∨
☐ Automatic Download 💡

[Advanced Dialog] [Get Media] [Cancel]

7 Click the **Get Media** button to download them

Hot tip

Images can also be downloaded from a USB flashdrive. To do this, connect the flashdrive and use the **From Camera or Card Reader...** download option. You will then be able to download the images in the same way as with a camera or memory card reader.

33

Hot tip

The Delete Options box in the Photo Downloader has options for what happens once you have downloaded your photos. These are: **After Copying, Do Not Delete Originals**; **After Copying, Verify and Delete Originals**; and **After Copying, Delete Originals**. If you do delete the originals from your camera or card reader, make sure you back up the ones that you have just downloaded, to a USB flashdrive or an external hard drive.

...cont'd

 Click on the **Advanced Dialog** button to access
additional options for downloading your images. Here, you can select specific images so that they are not all downloaded at once

The Advanced Dialog Photo Downloader has an option to **Automatically Fix Red Eyes**. Check this box **On** if you want red-eye to be removed from photos as they are downloaded.

Depending on the number of photos that you have on your camera or memory card, the downloading process may take a few minutes.

 Click on the **Get Media** button to import the images. They can then be viewed in the Organizer and opened in the Editor

Get Media

Click on the **Minimize** button in Step 9 so that you can get on with other tasks while your photos are being downloaded.

Copying - 3% Completed

From: **E:\<Camera or Card Reader>**
To: C:\Users\Nick\Pictures\2017 09 18

3%

File 40 of 1293: Copying File...

DSC_0513.JPG

Minimize   Stop

Importing in bulk

Using the Import function, it is also possible to import large numbers of images in one action, with the In Bulk... option:

 From the Organizer select **Import** > **In Bulk...**

Don't forget

By default, the main top-level folder (Pictures) is selected, and so are all of the sub-folders.

 In the **Import Media** window, you can select folders to import by checking the box next to them

Hot tip

Click on this button next to a folder (or sub-folder) to add the folder to a Watch List. This means that when new images are added to this folder on your computer, they will automatically be imported by Elements.

3 Click here to select a sub-folder

4 Check **Off** the main folder to deselect all sub-folders

5 Click on a specific sub-folder to select it. The main folder is also selected

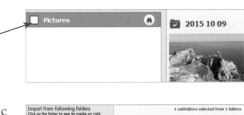

Don't forget

Even though the main folder becomes selected in Step 5, only one sub-folder is selected. This is shown at the top right-hand side of the window.

6 Click on the **Import** button to import the selected folders

35

Media View

Media View is the function within the Organizer that is used to view, find and sort images. When using Media View, images have to be actively added to it so it can then catalog them. Once images have been imported, Media View acts as a window for viewing and sorting your images, no matter where they are located. Media View is the default view when you access the Organizer and can be accessed at any time by clicking on the Media button:

Folders and Albums   Tag and Info panels

Organizer Taskbar   Keyword/Info button

There is also a magnification slider on the Taskbar, which can be used for changing the size at which images are viewed in the main Media View window:

Accessing images

To access images within Media View:

 Click on images to select them individually, or as a group (see second Hot tip)

 Drag the scroll bar to scroll through images within the main window

Double-click on an image to view it in the whole Media View window

Media View can be set to watch specific folders on your computer. Whenever images are added to these folders, or edited within them, you will be prompted to add them into the Media View. To specify the folders to be watched, select **File** > **Watch Folders** from the Menu bar and then browse to the folder, or folders, that you want to include.

Hot tip

When an Instant Fix is applied to a photo, a new photo is automatically created, and this is stored within a **Version Set** with the original photo. See page 41 for more details on Version Sets.

...cont'd

Media View functionality

Media View has a considerable amount of power and functionality in terms of organizing and editing images within the Organizer. This includes the Taskbar and panels for adding tags to images, and viewing information about them:

1 The Taskbar is located at the bottom of the main window and contains buttons for, from left to right: show or hide the Albums and Folders panel; undo the previous action; rotate a selected image; add images to a map for Places View; add an event to images for Event View; apply quick editing fixes; access the selected images in the Editor; view the selected images in a slideshow and access the Home Screen page

2 Select an image in the main Media View window and click on this button to apply instant editing fixes to it (without having to move to the Editor)

3 Click on one of the editing functions in the right-hand panel to apply it to the selected image(s)

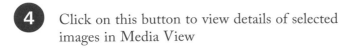

4 Click on this button to view details of selected images in Media View

5 Click on the **Information** tab. Click on these arrows to expand each section

Don't forget

For more details about adding tags to images, see pages 48-49.

6 Access the **General** panel to see information about the image name, size, date taken and where it is saved on your computer. You can edit the name and add a caption here

Hot tip

A caption can also be added to an image by selecting it and selecting **Edit > Add Caption** from the Menu bar.

7 Access the **Metadata** panel to see detailed information about an image that is added by the camera when it is taken

▼ Metadata
▼ FILE PROPERTIES
　　　　Filename: DSC_0516.JPG
Document Type: image/jpeg
　Date Created: 1/17/20...2:32 PM
　Date Modified: 1/17/20...2:38 PM
▼ CAMERA DATA (EXIF)
　　　　Make: NIKON ...RATION
　　　　Model: NIKON D3100
ISO Spe...atings: 200
　Exposure Time: 1/400 sec
　　　F-Stop: f/10
Focal Le...mm Film: 60
　Focal Length: 40.00 mm
　　　　Flash: Did not fire

Don't forget

Metadata is information about an image that is stored in the image file itself, in addition to the image that is displayed.

8 Click on this button to view an expanded list of Metadata information

9 Access the **History** panel to view the editing history of the image

▼ History
Modified Date: 1/17/2018 12:38 PM
　Imported On: 1/17/2018
Imported From: E:\<Camera or Card Reader>
　Volume Name: Acer

Stacks

Since digital cameras and smartphones make it quick, easy and cheap to capture dozens or hundreds of images, it is no surprise that most people are now capturing more images than ever before. One reason for this is that it is increasingly tempting to take several shots of the same subject, just to try to capture the perfect image. The one drawback with this is that when it comes to organizing your images on a computer, it can become time-consuming to work your way through all of your near-identical shots. Media View offers a useful solution to this by allowing you to stack similar images, so that you can view a single thumbnail rather than several. To do this:

Beware

You can remove images from a stack by selecting the stack in Media View and selecting **Edit** > **Stack** > **Flatten Stack** from the Menu bar. However, this will remove all of the images, apart from the top one, from Media View. This does not remove them from your hard drive, although there is an option to do this too, if you wish.

1 Select the images that you want to stack in Media View

2 Select **Edit** > **Stack** > **Stack Selected Photos** from the Menu bar

Don't forget

To revert stacked images to their original state, select the stack and select **Edit** > **Stack** > **Unstack Photos** from the Menu bar.

3 The images are stacked into a single thumbnail, and the existence of the stack is indicated by this icon

4 To view all of the stacked images, click this button

5 Click here to return to the rest of the photos in Media View

Beware

Only stack similar photos, otherwise you may forget which photos are underneath the stack.

Version Sets

When working with digital images it is commonplace to create several different versions of a single image. This could be to use one for printing and one for use on the web, or because there are elements of an image that you want to edit. Instead of losing track of images that have been edited, it is possible to create stacked thumbnails of edited images, which are known as Version Sets. These can include the original image and all of the edited versions. Version Sets can be created and added to from the Photo Editor and viewed in Media View. To do this:

The other Version Set menu options include **Flatten Version Set**, and **Revert to Original**. The latter deletes all of the other versions except the original image.

1 Open an image in the Photo Editor

2 Make editing changes to the image in either Expert edit mode or Quick edit mode

3 Select **File** > **Save As** from the Menu bar

4 Check on the **Save in Version Set with Original** box and click **Save**

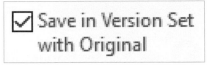

5 In Media View, the original image and the edited one are grouped together in a stack, and the fact that it is a Version Set is denoted by the icon in the top right-hand corner

Version Sets are also created if an image has an Instant Fix applied to it in the Organizer.

6 To view all of the images in a Version Set, select the set and select **Edit** > **Version Set** > **Expand Items in Version Set** from the Menu bar

People View

Shots of people are popular in most types of photography. However, this can result in hundreds or thousands of photos of different people. In Elements there is a feature that enables you to tag people throughout your collections. This is known as People Recognition. To use this:

Beware

Although People Recognition is very accurate, it may, at times, identify objects that are not faces at all.

1 In the Organizer, click on the **People** button, then click on the **Named** button

Hot tip

Select images by clicking and dragging over them, or holding down the **Ctrl** button (**Command** key on a Mac) and clicking on specific images.

2 Any named people are shown in the **Named** window

3 Click on the **Unnamed** button to view faces that have not already been assigned names

4 Click on one of the thumbnails to add a name

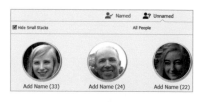

Don't forget

When you access a photo at full size in Media View, you will be prompted to add a person's name if there are people in the photo.

5 Add a name and click on the check mark symbol to apply the name to that group of photos

Adding people directly

To add names manually, directly from a photo:

1 Open a photo at full size in Media View and click on the **Mark Face** button

2 A prompt box appears on the screen. Drag this over the required face, add a name in the **Add Name** box and click on the green check mark to apply the name

Viewing people

To view people who have been tagged with People Recognition:

People Recognition really comes into its own when you have tagged dozens or hundreds of photos. You can then view all of the photos containing a specific person.

43

1 Click on the **People** button in the main Organizer window

2 Click on the **Named** button. The tagged people's photos are stacked in thumbnails. Click on a thumbnail to view all of the photos of that person (that have been tagged)

Double-click on the thumbnails in the Named window to view the images in a grid. In the grid, double-click on a single image to view it at full size.

Places View

One of the most common reasons for taking photos is when people are on vacation in different and new locations. Within the Organizer it is possible to tag photos to specific locations on a map, so that you can quickly view all of your photos from a certain area. To do this:

 In Media View, select all of the photos from a specific location

 On the Taskbar, click on the **Add Location** button

 Enter a location for the set of photos and click on the **Apply** button

To view photos that have been placed on a map, click on the **Places** button in the main Organizer window

You can move around the map by clicking and dragging. You can also zoom in and out by right-clicking on the map and selecting the relevant command.

Click on the **Unpinned** button at the top of the Places window to view all of the photos that have not had locations added to them. They appear next to the map so that they can be dragged onto a location.

5 Use these controls to move around the map
and zoom in and out on it

Hot tip

The map can be viewed
as **Map**, **Hybrid**, **Light**
or **Dark**. If **Map** is
selected, there is also
an option for viewing
Terrain.

6 Click on a set of photos in a
location. Click on this button
to move through them

7 Click on the **Edit** button to view the individual photos in
the left-hand panel

Beware

If a photo with an
existing location is
selected and the **Add
Location** button is
clicked, the location
for the photo can be
changed, but it will
be removed from the
original one.

8 Click on the **Done** button to exit the map

Events View

Photos in the Organizer can also be allocated to specific events such as family celebrations or overseas trips. This is done with the Events View. To do this:

When creating a new event, photos can be added to it by dragging them into the Media Bin below the window in Step 3.

When an event is created, the event name is automatically added to the tags, which can be accessed from the Media section in the Organizer.

Click on the "i" icon on the thumbnail in the Events window to see the description for that particular event.

 1 In Media View, select all of the required photos for a specific event

 2 On the Taskbar, click on the **Add Event** button

3 In the **Add New Event** panel, add details including name, start and end date, and a description of the event

 4 Click on the **Done** button

 5 To view photos that have been allocated to an event, click on the **Events** button in the main Organizer window

Events

6 All photos for a specific event are grouped together

7 Double-click on the thumbnail to view all of the photos allocated to the event

Hot tip

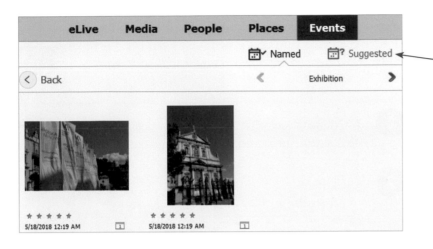

Click on the **Suggested** button at the top of the Events window to view groups of photos that Elements thinks may be suitable for new events.

 8 Click on the **Back** button to go back to the thumbnail view in Step 6

< Back

 9 Click on the **Calendar** to view events from specific dates

Calendar

Calendar		Clear
	All Years ▼	
Jan	Feb	Mar
Apr	May	Jun
Jul	Aug	Sep
Oct	Nov	Dec

Hot tip

Right-click on an event thumbnail to access a menu with options to edit the event; remove it; set it as a cover photo for the event thumbnail; or view it as a slideshow.

 10 Click on the **Add Event** button to create another event in Event View. This is done by dragging photos into the Media Bin and entering the event details as in Step 3

Add Event

Tagging Images

As your digital image collection begins to grow on your computer, it is increasingly important to be able to keep track of your images and find the ones you want, when you want them. One way of doing this is by assigning specific tags to images. You can then search for images according to the tags that have been added to them. The tagging function is accessed from the Tags panel within Media View in the Organizer. To add tags to images:

When you create a new category you can also choose a new icon.

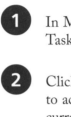 **1** In Media View, click on this button on the Taskbar to show and hide the Tags panel

Keyword/Info

2 Click here to access the currently-available tags

3 Click here to access sub-categories for a particular category

Tags can be created for People, Places and Events. They are also created when items are added to the various sections.

 4 Click here to add categories, or sub-categories, of your own choice

Tags are also referred to as Keywords or Keyword tags.

5 Enter a name for the new category, or sub-category, and click on the **OK** button

6 Select the required images from Media View

7 Drag a tag onto one of the selected images

8 The tag will be applied to all of the selected images. Each individual image will have the tag added to it

9 The images are tagged with the icon that denotes the main category, rather than the sub-category

Hot tip

Multiple tags can be added to the same image. This gives you greater flexibility when searching for images.

Don't forget

Categories can have several levels of sub-categories. To create additional levels, right-click on a sub-category and select **Create new Sub-Category** from the menu. Give the sub-category a name and ensure that the required item is selected in the **Parent Category or Sub-Category** box.

Don't forget

Tagged images can still be searched for using a sub-category tag, even though they are denoted in Media View by the tag for the main category.

49

Searching for Images

Once images have been tagged, they can then be searched for using those specific tags. To do this:

Using the Search box

Images can be searched for simply by typing keywords into the Search box at the top of the Organizer, in any view:

 Click on the Search button

 The Search window contains a Search box at the top of the window and also filter buttons down the left-hand side for conducting specific searches

50

After returning to Grid view in Step 4, click on the **Back** button to return to the main Organizer window. Click on the **Sort By:** box to sort the Search results according to Newest, Oldest, Name or Import Batch.

 Start typing in the Search box and click on one of the results to view all of the tagged images

 Click on the **Grid** button to view the images in the main Organizer window

Using search filters

The search filter buttons on the search page can also be used to find items. To do this:

1 Click on one of the search filter buttons to view the tagged photos, which are displayed according to their tags or categories. Click on one of the thumbnails in the left-hand panel to view the photos within it, displayed in the right-hand panel

The options for search filters are: Smart Tags; People; Places; Date; Folders; Keywords; Albums; Events; Ratings; and Media Types.

2 For each selection, the filter tag is added in the Search box. Add additional tags to create multiple searches to see all items that have two or more matching tags

...cont'd

Searching with tags

Images can also be searched for by using the tags within the Tags panel. To do this:

Tags can be viewed for **Keywords**, **People Tags**, **Places Tags** and **Events Tags**.

1 Access the Tags panel from this button

2 Check on a box to view the images that are tagged with that keyword

If you search using a main category, any items that are within that category as a sub-category will be searched for too. If you select a sub-category, this is only what will be searched for.

3 All matching items for a tag are shown together within the Media View window

Roll over a tag next to a photo in Media View to see a description of the Keyword tag.

4 Click on the **All Media** button to return to the rest of the images

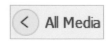

Multiple searches

Within the Tags panel it is also possible to define searches for images that have multiple (i.e. two or more) tags attached to them. To do this:

 Add a tag to an image or images, and click on the tag in the Tags panel to display all of these images (other tags that have been added to them will also be displayed next to the image)

 Add another tag to the image or images, so that there are at least two attached. Click on both of these in the Tags panel. Only the images containing both tags will be displayed

Albums

Albums in Elements are similar to physical photo albums: they are a location into which you can store all of your favorite groups of images. Once they have been stored there, they can easily be found when required. To create albums:

Don't forget

Version Sets and stacks can be added to and viewed in Albums.

Hot tip

Click on the New Album button in Step 1 to view options for collapsing or expanding all of the albums in the panel.

Don't forget

Right-click on an album name to access a menu with options to **Edit**, **Rename** or **Delete** the album.

1 In Media View, click here in the Albums panel and select **New Album**

2 Enter a name for the new album and choose a category if required

3 Select the images that you would like included in the new album and drag them into the Content panel

4 Click on the **OK** button

5 The selected images are placed into the new album. Click on an album to view the images within it

Folders

One important factor in storing and searching for photos is the use of folders. Elements can replicate the folder structure that you have on your hard drive and also create new folders and edit existing ones. To work with folders in Elements:

1 The available folders are listed next to the Albums section. Click on a folder to view its contents

2 New folders are created whenever you import photos into Elements using the **Import** > **From Files and Folders...** command

3 In hierarchy view, right-click on a folder to access the available options for editing it or adding a new folder

Auto Curate

Since it is easy to take hundreds or thousands of photos with a digital camera or smartphone, it can become slightly overwhelming in terms of sorting out the best ones. Within the Organizer there is a function that does this for you, by selecting the best range of photos for specific selections. This is known as Auto Curate. To use this:

1 Open the Organizer and select a group of photos, either as an Album, a Folder or by using a Keyword tag

Auto Curate requires a minimum of 10 photos in a group in order to perform its selection.

2 Check the **Auto Curate** box (above the Keywords and Info panels) to On

If no selection is made in Step 1, Auto Curate will search over 500 photos to find the best ones.

3 Auto Curate selects what it thinks are the best photos from the group

4 Drag the slider to show more or fewer photos for the Auto Curate selection

Check Off the **Auto Curate** box to return to the original view.

Opening and Saving Images

Once you have captured images with a digital camera, smartphone, or a scanner and stored them on your computer, you can open them in any of Elements' Editor modes. There are a number of options for this:

Open command

 Select **File** > **Open** from the Menu bar, or click on the **Open** button and select an option

 Select an image from your hard drive and click **Open**

Open As command

This can be used to open a file in a different file format to its original. To do this:

 Select **File** > **Open As** from the Menu bar

 Select an image and select the file format. Click **Open**

Saving images

When saving digital images, it is always a good idea to save them in at least two different file formats, particularly if layered objects such as text and shapes have been added. One of these formats should be the proprietary Photoshop format PSD or PDD. The reason for using this is that it will retain all of the layered information within an image. So, if a text layer has been added, it will still be available for editing once it has been saved and closed.

The other format that an image should be saved in is the one most appropriate for the use to which it is going to be put. Therefore, images that are going to be used on the web should be saved as JPEG, GIF or PNG files, while an image that is going to be used for printing should be saved in another format, such as TIFF. Once images have been saved in these formats, all of the layered information within them becomes flattened into a single layer and it will not be possible to edit these individual layers.

Another option for opening files is the **Open Recently Edited File** command, which is accessed from the File menu. This lists, in order, the files you have opened most recently. Some of these are also listed on the **Open** button's drop-down menu.

A proprietary file format is one that is specific to the program being used. It has greater flexibility when used within the program itself, but cannot be distributed as easily as other images.

The **Save As** command should be used if you want to make a copy of an image with a different file name.

Working with Video

As well as using Elements for viewing and organizing photos, it can also be used in the same way with video. Video can be imported into Elements in a number of ways:

Elements Premiere can be bought as a package with Elements, or it can be bought individually.

- From a camera that has video-recording capabilities.

- From a digital video camera.

- From a smartphone.

- From video that has been created in the Elements Premiere program. This is a companion program to Elements and is used to manipulate and edit video. It can be bought in a package with Elements, or individually. For more details see **www.adobe.com/products/premiere-elements/**

To download video into Elements:

Beware

Video files are usually much larger in size than photos, and if you have lots of them they will take up a lot of space on your computer.

1 Connect the device containing the video. In the Organizer, click on the **Import** button, select the required device and download in the same way as for photos

Don't forget

To view video clips, double-click on the clip in Media View. The Elements video player will open and play the video clip.

2 The video is downloaded and displayed in the Organizer, in the same way as photos

Don't forget

To find video clips within Elements, select **Find > By Media Type > Video** from the Menu bar, and the video files will be displayed.

3 Video clips are identified by this symbol on their thumbnails in Media View in the Organizer

3 First Digital Steps

This chapter shows how to get up and running with digital image editing, and details some effective editing techniques for improving digital images, such as improving overall color and duplicating items.

Hot tip

Another Auto command on the Enhance menu is Auto Smart Fix. This can be used to automatically edit all of the color balance of an image in one step. This is also available as a panel in Quick edit mode.

Hot tip

The keyboard shortcut for Auto Levels is:
PC: Shift + Ctrl + L
Mac: Shift + Command
        key + L

The keyboard shortcut for Auto Contrast is:
PC: Alt + Shift + Ctrl
        + L
Mac: Alt + Shift +
        Command key + L

Hot tip

Two other options for color enhancement in the Toolbox are the Burn tool and the Dodge tool. The Burn tool can be dragged over areas in an image to make them darker, and the Dodge tool can be dragged over areas to make them lighter.

Color Enhancements

Some of the simplest but most effective editing changes that can be made to digital images are color enhancements. These can help to transform a mundane image into a stunning one, and Elements offers a variety of methods for achieving this. Some of these are verging towards the professional end of image editing, while others are done almost automatically by Elements. These are known as Auto adjustments, and some simple manual adjustments can also be made to the brightness and contrast of an image. All of these color enhancement features can be accessed from the Enhance menu on the Menu bar, in both Expert and Quick edit modes.

Auto Levels

This automatically adjusts the overall color tone of an image in relation to the lightest and darkest points in the image:

Auto Contrast

This automatically adjusts the contrast of an image:

Auto Color Correction

This automatically adjusts all of the color elements within an image:

Hot tip

The keyboard shortcut for Auto Color Correction is Shift + Ctrl + B (Shift + Command key + B on a Mac).

Adjust Brightness/Contrast

This can be used to manually adjust the brightness and contrast in an image:

1 Select **Enhance** > **Adjust Lighting** > **Brightness/Contrast** from the Menu bar (in either Expert or Quick edit mode)

2 Drag the sliders to adjust the image's brightness and contrast

3 Click on the **OK** button

4 The brightness and contrast (and a range of other color editing functions) can also be adjusted using the panels in Quick edit mode

Don't forget

Alter the brightness and contrast by small amounts at a time when you are editing an image. This will help ensure that the end result does not look too unnatural.

61

Hot tip

Always make sure that the Preview box is checked when you are applying color enhancements. This will display the changes as you make them, and before they are applied to the image.

Hot tip

Adjusting shadows can make a significant improvement to an image in which one area is under-exposed and the rest is correctly exposed.

Don't forget

Shadows and highlights can also be adjusted in the Levels panel: **Enhance** > **Adjust Color** > **Levels** from the Menu bar. See pages 116-119 for more details about Levels.

Beware

Some digital cameras have a tendency to create slightly darker images, so adjusting the Shadows/Highlights is always a good option.

...cont'd

Adjust Shadows/Highlights

One problem that most photographers encounter at some point is when part of an image is exposed correctly, while another part is either over- or under-exposed. If this is corrected using general color correction techniques such as adjusting levels of brightness and contrast, the poorly-exposed area may be improved, but at the expense of the area that was correctly exposed initially. To overcome this, the Shadows/Highlights command can be used to adjust particular tonal areas of an image. To do this:

1 Open an image where parts of the image, or all of it, are incorrectly exposed

2 Select **Enhance** > **Adjust Lighting** > **Shadows/ Highlights** from the Menu bar

3 Make the required adjustments by dragging the sliders

4 Click on the **OK** button

5 The poorly-exposed areas of the image have been corrected

Cropping

Cropping is a technique that can be used to remove unwanted areas of an image and highlight the main subject. The area to be cropped can only be selected as a rectangle. To crop an image:

 Select the **Crop** tool from the Toolbox

 Click and drag on an image to select the area to be cropped. The area that is selected is retained and the area to be cropped appears grayed-out

3 Click and drag on these markers to resize the crop area

4 Click on the check mark to accept the changes, or the circle to reject them

The different crop options are all accessed from the Tool Options bar.

The Tool Options for the Crop tool have an option for selecting pre-set sizes for the Crop tool. This results in the crop being in specific proportions; e.g. 10 x 8 inches. Click on the down-pointing arrow in the No Restriction box and select an option.

When cropping photos it is also possible to use various overlay grids to help the composition of the image. One of these is the Rule of Thirds, whereby the cropped area is based on a 3x3 grid, with the main subjects positioned at the intersecting points of the gridlines.

63

...cont'd

Perspective cropping

Due to the way some lenses are constructed on digital cameras, tall buildings can sometimes look distorted (and also at slight angles). This can be amended using the Perspective Crop tool:

Don't forget

To simplify the crop function, there are a range of auto crop options, where the suggested crop area is displayed using a range of preset options. To use these, select the **Crop** tool. The auto crop options are displayed on four buttons in the Tool Options panel. Click on an option to select it and click on the green check mark to accept the suggested crop area, or click on the red circle to reject the suggestion.

1   Open the image to be amended

2   Select the **Perspective Crop** tool from the Crop Tool Options

3   Drag the Perspective Crop tool around the required area, in the same way as for a regular crop

4   Drag the top corners of the crop area to specify the dimensions for the selected area (dragging the corners outwards narrows the perspective). Click on the green check mark symbol to apply the perspective crop

Healing Brush

One of the most popular techniques in digital imaging is removing unwanted items, particularly physical blemishes such as spots and wrinkles. This can be done with the Clone tool but the effects can sometimes be too harsh, as a single area is copied over the affected item. A more subtle effect can be achieved with the Healing Brush and the Spot Healing Brush tools. The Healing Brush can be used to remove blemishes over larger areas such as wrinkles:

The Healing Brush tool can be more subtle than the Clone tool, as it blends the copied area together with the area over which it is copying. This is particularly effective on images of people, as it preserves the overall skin tone better than the Clone tool does.

1 Open an image with blemishes covering a reasonably large area; i.e. more than a single spot

2 Select the **Healing Brush** tool from the Toolbox and make the required selections in the Tool Options bar

The Spot Healing Brush tool can be used to remove items such as small blemishes or spots. Click on this button in the Healing Brush Tool Options bar and drag it over the affected area to remove it.

3 Hold down **Alt** and click on an area of the image to load the Healing Brush tool. Drag over the affected area. The cross is the area that is copied beneath the circle. At this point the overall tone is not perfect and looks too pink

4 Release the mouse, and the Healing Brush blends the affected area with the one that was copied over it. This creates a much more natural skin tone

When dragging over a blemish with the Spot Healing Brush tool, make sure the brush size is larger than the area of the blemish. This will ensure that you can cover the blemish in a single stroke.

Cloning

Cloning is a technique that can be used to copy one area of an image over another. This can be used to cover up small imperfections in an image, such as a dust mark or a spot, and also to copy or remove large items in an image, such as a person.

To clone items:

1 Select the **Clone Stamp** tool from the Toolbox

2 Set the Clone Stamp options in the Tool Options bar

3 Hold down **Alt**, and then click and hold on the image to select a source point from which the cloning will start

4 Drag the cursor to copy everything over which the selection point marker passes

Pattern Cloning

The Pattern Stamp tool can be used to copy a selected pattern over an image, or onto a selected area of an image. To do this:

1 Select the **Pattern Stamp** tool from the Toolbox

2 Click here in the Tool Options bar to access the available patterns

The Pattern Stamp tool is grouped in the Toolbox with the Clone Stamp tool. It can be selected from the Tool Options panel if the Clone Stamp tool is selected.

3 Select a pattern for the Pattern Stamp tool

4 Click and drag on an image to copy the selected pattern over it

Patterns can be added to the Patterns panel by selecting an image, or an area of an image, and selecting **Edit** > **Define Pattern** from the Editor Menu bar. Then, give the pattern a name in the **Pattern Name** dialog box, and click **OK**.

Rotating

Various rotation commands can be applied to images, and also individual layers in layered images. This can be useful for positioning items and also for correcting the orientation of an image that is on its side or upside down.

Rotating a whole image

1 Select **Image** > **Rotate** from the Menu bar

2 Select a rotation option from the menu

3 Select **Custom...** to enter your own value for the amount you want an image rotated

4 Click the **OK** button

Rotating a layer
To rotate separate layers within an image:

1 Open an image that consists of two or more layers. Select one of the layers in the Layers panel

2 Select **Image** > **Rotate** from the Menu bar

3 Select a layer rotation option from the menu

4 The selected layer is rotated independently

Transforming

The Transform commands can be used to resize an image, and to apply some basic distortion techniques. These commands can be accessed by selecting **Image** > **Transform** from the Menu bar.

Free Transform

This enables you to manually alter the size and shape of an image. To do this:

 Select **Image** > **Transform** > **Free Transform** from the Menu bar

Click and drag here to transform the vertical and horizontal size of the image. Hold down **Shift** to transform it in proportion

Click just outside this placeholder and drag left or right to manually rotate an image with the Transform function.

The other options from the Transform menu are Skew, Distort and Perspective. These can be accessed and applied in a similar way to the Free Transform option.

Magnification

In Elements there are a number of ways in which the magnification at which an image is being viewed can be increased or decreased. This can be useful if you want to zoom in on a particular part of an image for editing purposes, or if you want to view a whole image to see the result of editing effects that have been applied.

View menu

Don't forget

The View menu can be used to display rulers at the top and left of an image, which can be useful for precise measurements and placement. There is also a command for displaying a grid over the top of the whole image.

 Select **View** from the Menu bar and select one of the options from the View menu

View	Window	Help
New Window for bulgaria4.jpg		
Zoom In		Ctrl+=
Zoom Out		Ctrl+-
Fit on Screen		Ctrl+0
Actual Pixels		Ctrl+1
Print Size		
Selection		Ctrl+H
Rulers		Shift+Ctrl+R
Grid		Ctrl+'

Zoom tool

Hot tip

The keyboard shortcut for zooming in is:
PC: Ctrl + =
Mac: Command key + =

The keyboard shortcut for zooming out is:
PC: Ctrl + -
Mac: Command key + -

 Select the **Zoom** tool from the Toolbox

 Click once on an image to enlarge it (usually by 100% each time). Hold down **Alt** and click to decrease the magnification

Hot tip

Click and drag with the Zoom tool over a small area to increase the magnification to the maximum; i.e. 3200%. This can be particularly useful when performing close-up editing tasks, such as removing red-eye.

...cont'd

Navigator panel
This can be used to move around an image and also magnify certain areas. To use the Navigator panel:

 1 Access the **Navigator** panel by selecting **Window** > **Navigator** from the Menu bar

2 Drag this slider to magnify the area of the image within the red rectangle

3 Drag the rectangle to change the area of the image that is being magnified

The keyboard shortcut for accessing the Navigator panel is F12.

The Navigator panel also has buttons for zooming in and out. These are located at the left and right of the slider.

71

Click on different areas on the thumbnail in the Navigator panel to view these areas in the main Editor window.

Eraser

The Eraser tool can be used to remove areas of an image. In a simple, single-layer image this can just leave a blank hole, which has to be filled with something. The Eraser options are:

- **Eraser**, which can be used to erase part of the background image or a layer within it.

- **Background Eraser**, which can be used to remove an uneven background.

- **Magic Eraser**, which can be used to quickly remove a solid background (see below).

Erasing a background

With the Magic Eraser tool it is possible to delete a colored background in an image. To do this:

The Background Eraser tool can be used to remove an uneven background. To do this, drag over the background with the Background Eraser tool and, depending on the settings in the Tool Options panel, everything that it is dragged over will be removed.

1 Open an image with an evenly-colored background

2 Select the **Magic Eraser** and make the required selections in the Tool Options bar. Make sure the Contiguous box is not checked

3 Click once on the background. It is removed from the image, regardless of where it occurs

If the **Contiguous** box is not checked, the background color will be removed wherever it occurs in the image. If the Contiguous box is checked, the background color will only be removed where it touches another area of the same color that is not broken by another element of the image.

4 Quick Wins

This chapter looks at some of the "quick wins" that can be done in Elements, such as removing unwanted objects, changing photos to black and white, and improving hazy photos. It also shows some of the Guided and Quick edit options that provide step-by-step actions for creating a range of creative and striking photos. This includes adding items to photos, such as filters and graphics and creating panoramas.

Removing Red-Eye

One of the most common problems with photographs of people, whether they are taken digitally or with a film-based camera, is red-eye. This is caused when the camera's flash is used, which then reflects in the subject's pupils. This can create the dreaded red-eye effect, where the subject can unintentionally be transformed into a demonic character.

Elements has recognized that removing red-eye is one of the top priorities for most amateur photographers, and a specific tool for this purpose has been included in the Toolbox: the Eye Tool. This is available in Expert or Quick edit modes:

The best way to deal with red-eye is to avoid it in the first place. Try using a camera that has a red-eye reduction function.

Don't forget

There is also an option in the Eye tool for removing red-eye from pets.

Don't forget

Red-eye can also be removed when images are being downloaded from the camera. This is an option in the Photo Downloader window.

Hot tip

Red-eye can be removed automatically by clicking on the **Auto Correct** button in the Eye tool Options panel.

1 Open an image that contains red-eye

2 Select the **Zoom** tool from the Toolbox

3 Drag around the affected area until it appears at a suitable magnification. Select the **Eye** tool from the Toolbox

4 Click in the Tool Options bar to select the size of the pupil and the amount by which it will be darkened

Pupil Radius: 50%
Darken: 50%

5 Click once on the red-eye, or drag around the affected area to remove the red-eye

Red Eye Removal

Auto Correct

Changing to Black and White

Most digital cameras and scanners are capable of converting color images into black and white at the point of capture. However, it is also possible to use Elements to convert existing color images into black-and-white ones. To do this:

 Open a color image and select **Enhance > Convert to Black and White** from the Menu bar

 The Convert to Black and White dialog box has various options for how the image is converted

Select the type of black-and-white effect to be applied, depending on the subject in the image

Drag these sliders to specify the intensity of the effect to be applied for different elements

Click on the **OK** button

 The image is converted into black and white, according to the settings that have been selected

The keyboard shortcut to access the Convert to Black and White dialog window is Alt + Ctrl + B (Alt + Command key + B on a Mac).

A similar effect can be achieved by selecting **Enhance > Adjust Color > Remove Color** from the Menu bar.

The Guided edits also have an option for turning photos into black and white: **Guided > Black & White > Black and White**.

Quickly Removing Items

One of the most annoying aspects of taking photos is to capture what you think is a perfect image, only to find that there is an unwanted object in the final shot. In Elements, it is possible to delete unwanted items and automatically fill in the area from where these are removed. To do this:

Don't forget

Several different items can be removed from the same photo. To do this, select each one separately and perform the actions from Step 3 onwards.

Hot tip

The selection around the object does not have to be too accurate, as long as it goes around the border of the object.

Beware

If an area is selected and then deleted it will leave a blank space, filled with either the color palette's background or foreground color.

1 Open an image that contains an unwanted object

2 Use one of the selection tools to select the unwanted object

3 Select **Edit > Fill Selection...** from the Menu bar

Edit	Image	Enhance	Layer
Undo Lasso			Ctrl+Z
Redo Fill			Ctrl+Y
Revert			Shift+Ctrl+A
Cut			Ctrl+X
Copy			Ctrl+C
Copy Merged			Shift+Ctrl+C
Paste			Ctrl+V
Paste Into Selection			Shift+Ctrl+V
Delete			
Fill Selection...			

4 Make the selections in the Fill Layer dialog box. Ensure **Content-Aware** is selected

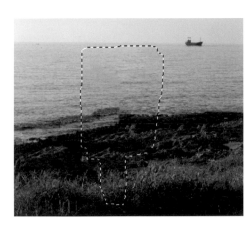

5 Click on the **OK** button

6 The selection is deleted and the area is automatically filled with the background

Beware

If there are too many colors around the selected area, the fill effect may appear inaccurate. If this is the case, try with a slightly different selection area.

7 The final image makes it appear as if the unwanted object was never there in the first place

Don't forget

Zoom in to the final image to make sure that the background has been filled as accurately as possible.

Moving Items in a Photo

Unless you are taking photos under studio conditions, it is probable that you will get some unwanted items in your photos, or the composition may not be exactly as you would like it in terms of the position of the subjects. The answer to this is the Content-Aware editing tool. This can be used to move subjects in a photo and then have the background behind them filled in automatically.

In the Content-Aware Move Options panel, drag the **Healing** slider to specify how the edited area blends with the rest of the image.

1 Open an image with a subject that you want to move

2 Select the **Content-Aware Move** tool from the Toolbox

3 Select the **Move** radio button in Tool Options

4 Drag around the subject that you want to move

When moving items, it is most effective when the background has a reasonable amount of solid or similar colors.

The Content-Aware Move selection area can be moved by using the arrow keys on the keyboard; e.g. left and right, up and down.

5 Drag the subject to a new position

The subject can be positioned anywhere in the photo.

6 The area where the subject was previously located is filled in by the Content-Aware function

The Content-Aware tool can also be used to extend areas within an image. To do this, check on the **Extend** box in Tool Options, drag around the area you want to extend, and then drag the selection into place. The Content-Aware Move tool will automatically fill in the background for the area that is extended.

Improving Expressions

Taking photos of people is a very common use for digital cameras. However, sometimes the end result is not quite as expected: perhaps the subject is not smiling enough, or has their eyes half-closed. In Elements 2019 it is possible to adjust these imperfections so that all of your portraits look their best. To do this:

Don't forget

The circle around the face in Step 1 is preset and cannot be moved or resized. It serves to show the face that is selected.

Beware

Make small facial adjustments at a time, otherwise the final image may end up looking like a caricature.

Hot tip

If there is more than one person in a photo, click on each one to select them and adjust their features. Only one person can be selected at a time, and when they are selected, the circle in Step 1 appears around their face.

Don't forget

Click on the **Reset** button to return to the original, unaltered image.

Reset

1 Open the image containing the expression that you want to edit. In either Quick or Expert edit mode, select **Enhance > Adjust Facial Features** from the Menu bar

2 Drag the sliders to amend the elements of the facial expression. This can be done for **Lips**, **Eyes**, **Nose** and **Face** options

3 As the changes are made, they are reflected in the subject's face (if the **After** button is selected)

4 Click on the **OK** button to apply the facial adjustment changes

OK

Removing Haze

Despite our best efforts, some photos do not come out the way we hoped. One problem can be that photos appear hazy, which is often accompanied by a washed-out sky. To remedy this:

 Open a photo that is suffering from a hazy effect

Select **Enhance > Haze Removal** from the Menu bar in Expert or Quick edit mode

The Haze Removal window displays the image

Drag this slider to apply the haze removal effect

Drag this slider to apply the degree of the effect

Haze removal is a good option for landscape photos that have been taken in dull lighting.

Toggle the **Before/ After** button at the bottom of the Haze Removal window to view the two states of the image.

There is also an Auto Haze Removal option that can be accessed from the Menu bar in Expert or Quick edit mode: **Enhance > Auto Haze Removal**.

81

Opening Closed Eyes

Taking photos of people can be a frustrating business: you think you have captured the perfect shot, only to find that one or more of your subjects has their eyes closed. Thankfully, with Elements 2019 these types of photos can be edited by opening any closed eyes in the shot. To do this:

82

1 Open a photo that has a subject with closed eyes

2 Select **Enhance** > **Open Closed Eyes** from the Menu bar in Expert or Quick edit mode

3 Select a location to choose an image with open eyes for the subject; e.g. the Organizer or from your computer

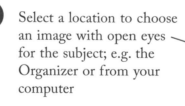

4 Select the required images and click on the **Add Selected Photos** button

Add Selected Photos

Click on the **Done** button

 The selected images are added to the Eye Source panel

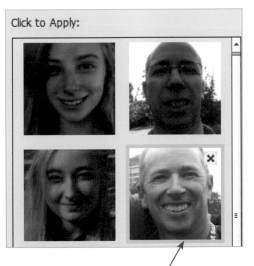

Don't forget

All of the people included in the images selected in Step 4 are included in the Eye Source panel.

Click on a suitable image with open eyes for the subject

The selection from the Eye Source panel replaces the closed eyes of the subject

Hot tip

Once new eyes have been added to a subject, they can also be edited using the Adjust Facial Features function (see page 80), or normal image-editing functions, such as the Spot Healing Brush or cloning.

 Click on the **Reset** button to start again, or the **OK** button to apply the change

Auto Creations are a new feature in Elements 2019.

Auto Creations are created from Events that have been created in Elements 2019, and also from photos that were taken on the same date.

Auto Creations

Organizing and editing photos so that you have a creative and entertaining slideshow to show family and friends can be time-consuming and frustrating. Selected groups of photos can be played as slideshows, but Elements 2019 has a more powerful function: Auto Creations.

Auto Creations is an automatic function within Elements 2019 that creates artistic slideshows and collages (including transitions between photos and background music). They can be viewed directly from the Home Screen and also deleted or edited, as required. To use Auto Creations:

 Click on the **Home Screen** button on either the Photo Editor or Organizer bottom Taskbar

 Auto Creations are displayed in their own panel on the Home Screen

 Click here to view the top five Auto Creations on the Home Screen

 Click on the **View All** button to view all of the available Auto Creations

5 Click on the **Trash** icon next to an Auto Creation to delete it

6 On the Home Screen, or in the View All section, click on the **Open** button to view an Auto Creation. If it is a slideshow, it starts playing in its own window

Don't forget

If the Auto Creation is a collage, it will be opened in the Quick Edit section of the Photo Editor, see page 87 for details.

7 Click on the **Back** button to go back to the Organizer

8 Click on these button on the left-hand toolbar to, from top to bottom: add more photos or videos to the Auto Creation and add captions to existing items; change the theme for the Auto Creation; and edit the music being used (see pages 86-87 for more information about editing Auto Creations)

Don't forget

If the Auto Creation has not been saved, you will be prompted to do this when the Back button is clicked in Step 7.

9 Click on these buttons at the top of the window to **Save** an Auto Creation to the Organizer, or **Export** it to a social media site or to a location on your own computer

Beware

Until an Auto Creation has been saved, it is only available from the Home Screen. Once it has been saved it can also be opened from the Organizer mode.

...cont'd

Editing Slideshow Auto Creations

If an Auto Creation has been opened as a slideshow, it can be edited from within the Slideshow window where it is played, as shown on page 85. To do this:

Click on this button to the right of the caption button in Step 1 to add more photos or videos to the slideshow.

1 Click on the **Media** button and click here to add captions below each photo

Don't forget

Themes are added to the whole slideshow, rather than to individual photos.

2 Click on the **Themes** button to select a background color theme for the slideshow

Beware

If too many different music tracks are added to an Auto Creation slideshow it can make it feel slightly disjointed.

3 Click on the **Audio** button to select music for the slideshow. Click on an item here to add it

Editing Collage Auto Creations

If an Auto Creations has been opened as a collage, it is opened in the Photo Editor, where it can be edited and then saved as a new project. To do this:

 Click on the **Open** button next to a collage on the Home Screen

 The collage opens in Photo Editor mode

 Click on these buttons to add more photos to the collage, from your computer or the Elements Organizer

87

Hot tip

The graphical elements in Step 5 include backgrounds and frames.

Click the **Layouts** button on the bottom taskbar and click on one of the layouts to apply it to the collage

Landscape

Don't forget

Click on the **Save** button on the bottom taskbar to save the current collage to the Organizer, whether it has been edited or not.

Click the **Graphics** button on the bottom taskbar and click on one of the graphical elements to add it to the collage

Backgrounds

Save

Quick Edit Mode Options

The Quick edit options in Elements offer a number of functions within the one location. This makes it easier to apply a number of techniques at the same time.

Using Quick edit mode

Quick edit mode is a good way to view how certain editing functions are applied automatically. Once you are confident with this, you can use Expert edit mode to perform similar tasks manually, which can give you more control over the final effects.

 Open an image in the Editor and click on the **Quick** button

 The Quick edit mode has a modified Toolbox with fewer tools, which is displayed here

 Click on the bottom toolbar to access the Quick edit panel options. The default one is for **Adjustments**

Click on the **Adjustments** panel to make the appropriate changes (see pages 90-91)

The other Quick edit panels are: **Effects**, **Textures** and **Frames**, which can be used to add graphical elements to an image.

Quick Edit Toolbox

The Quick edit Toolbox has a reduced Toolbox that includes:

- Zoom tool
- Hand tool

- Quick Selection tool
- Eye tool
- Whiten Teeth tool
- Straighten tool
- Text tool
- Spot Healing/Healing tool
- Crop tool
- Move tool

Hot tip

To show or hide the Quick edit Toolbox (and also the Expert edit Toolbox) select **Window** > **Tools** from the Menu bar.

Whitening teeth

One of the tool options in the Quick edit mode Toolbox is for whitening teeth in a photo. To do this:

Beware

The Eye tool is the same as the one in Expert mode, which includes the Pet Eye option for removing red-eye in photos of pets.

1 Open a relevant image and click on the **Whiten Teeth** tool, and select a brush size for the tool

2 Drag the Whiten Teeth tool over the teeth

3 The teeth area is selected and whitened in one operation

Beware

Do not overdo the teeth whitening effect, otherwise it will start to look unnatural.

Quick Edit Adjustments

The adjustment panels in the Quick edit section are:

Changes are displayed in the main Quick edit window in real time, as they are being made.

Smart Fix panel

This performs several editing changes in a single operation. Click on the Auto button to have the changes applied automatically, or drag the slider to specify the extent of the editing changes. Click on the thumbnails to apply preset amounts of the change.

Hot tip

The Exposure panel is a good option for quickly editing photos that are under- or over-exposed; i.e. too dark or too light.

Exposure panel

This provides options for adjusting the lighting and contrast in an image. Drag the sliders to adjust the exposure, or click on one of the thumbnails to apply a preset option.

Don't forget

Shadows and highlights can be edited within Expert edit mode: **Enhance** > **Adjust Lighting** > **Shadows/ Highlights**.

Lighting panel

This provides options for adjusting the lightest and darkest points in an image. This is done by adjusting the shadows, midtones and highlights. Drag the slider to adjust this, or click on one of the thumbnails for an auto option.

Color panel

Click on the Auto button to automatically adjust the hue and saturation of an image, or drag the slider to make manual adjustments. Click on the thumbnails to apply preset amounts.

Balance panel

Drag the slider to adjust the warmth of the colors of an image and the color balance. Click on the thumbnails to apply preset amounts.

Sharpen panel

This can be used to apply sharpening to an image to make it clearer: either automatically with the Auto button; with the panel thumbnails; or manually with the slider.

The Balance panel can be used to create some abstract color effects.

Sharpening works by increasing the contrast between adjoining pixels to make the overall image appear more in focus. It can also be accessed by selecting **Enhance** > **Auto Sharpen** or **Enhance** > **Unsharp Mask** from the Expert Menu bar. The Unsharp Mask option has a dialog window where the effect can be added as a percentage.

91

Adding Filters

Filters are an excellent option for adding a range of effects to photos. They can be accessed and applied from the Menu bar in Expert or Quick edit mode, or the toolbar in Expert edit mode:

Each preset option overrides any previous ones that have been selected; they do not build up on top of each other.

1 In Expert edit mode, open the photo to which you want to apply a filter effect, and click on the **Filters** panel button

2 Click on a filter effect and use the sliders to determine the settings for the filter. Click on the green check mark symbol to apply the filter effect

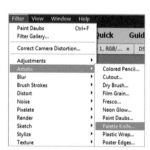

92

The most recently used filter can be reapplied by pressing Ctrl + F on the keyboard (Command key + F on a Mac).

3 Alternatively, in Expert or Quick edit mode, click on the **Filter** button on the Menu bar, and select a filter category and sub-category

Use the Unsharp Mask filter to sharpen the focus of a photo. Although this is a filter, it is accessed from **Enhance > Unsharp Mask** on the Menu bar. In the **Amount** box, drag the slider to apply the amount of sharpening: a value of 100% or above is effective in most cases.

4 Each category has preset options. Click on one to apply this to the photo

5 Most filters have sliders that can be used to edit the effect that is being applied. After you have made the desired changes, click on the **OK** button

Adding Graphics

In Expert edit mode it is possible to add a wide range of graphical elements to an image. To do this:

1 Click on the **Graphics** panel button

2 At the top of the Graphics panel, click on the **Show All** drop-down menus to select categories and sub-categories

Show All

Backgrounds
Frames
Graphics
Shapes
Text
Show All

Show All

By Type
By Activity
By Color
By Event
By Mood
By Object
By Seasons
By Style
By Word
Show All

93

Beware

There are hundreds of graphics that can be used, but try not to add too many to a single image as it may become too cluttered.

3 Graphical shapes can be dragged onto an image, on a new layer, and then resized within the image by clicking on them and dragging the resizing handles

Hot tip

Click on the **Layers** panel button after graphics have been added to see how this affects the construction of the image.

4 Backgrounds can be dragged onto an image as a new layer, and the rest of the content can interact with the background through the application of layer masks or opacity (see pages 144-147)

Using Guided Edit Mode

In Elements, the Guided edit function makes it easier to perform both simple editing functions, and also more complex image-editing processes that consist of a number of steps. To use the various functions of Guided edit mode:

94

1 Open an image and click on the **Guided** button

2 Click on the buttons at the top of the Guided edits window to view the different categories

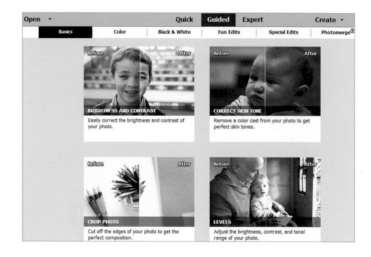

3 Items in each category have a thumbnail image that shows the **Before** and **After** effects for each item. Drag the slider across the thumbnail to view the effect for a greater or lesser amount of the thumbnail

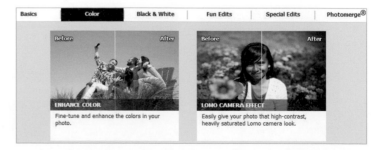

Applying Guided edits

The process for Guided edits is the same regardless of the type of edit that has been selected:

1 Apply the Guided edit effect that has been selected. Different categories have varying numbers of steps; the **Basics** category has the fewest number of steps

For details of some of the Guided edit options, see Chapter 5.

2 Click on the **Next** button once the Guided edits have been completed, to save the final image

If you do not like an effect that has been applied, click on the **Cancel** button.

3 Specify how you want to save and/or share the final image

Click on the **Save** button to save the final image with the same file name, and in the same file format (this overwrites the original). Click on the **Save As** button to save it as a new image with either a new file name or in a new file format, or both.

4 Click on the **Done** button

Photomerge Effects

Within Elements there are a number of Photomerge effects that can be used to combine elements from different photos to create a new image. This can be used to remove items from photos, combine elements from two or more photos, and match the exposure from different photos.

To access the Photomerge options, select **Guided** edit mode and click on the **Photomerge** tab.

The Photomerge options are:

- **Compose**. This can be used to merge a part of one image with the background of another. This is a good option if you want to include people from one photo and transfer them into another photo.

- **Exposure**. This can be used to create a well-exposed photo from a series of photos of the same shot that have different exposures; i.e. one may be over-exposed and another under-exposed. The Photomerge effect combines the photos so that the final one is correctly exposed. This can be done with the **Automatic** option, or the **Manual** one.

- **Faces**. This is an option for combining features of two faces together. This is done by opening photos of two people and then aligning the features of one so that they are merged with the other. This is a fun effect that can be used to combine faces of family members or two friends.

- **Group Shot**. This can be used to add or delete people from group shots. This is done by opening two or more photos of the group. Use the **Pencil** tool to merge a person from one photo into the other, and the **Eraser** tool to delete any areas that you do not want copied to the new photo.

- **Scene Cleaner**. This can be used to remove any unwanted elements in a photo. This is done by using two or more similar photos with elements that you want to remove, then merging the elements that you want to keep into the final photo. This is a good option if a single object has spoilt what is otherwise a good photo.

- **Panorama**. This can be used to create panoramas with two or more photos (see pages 97-98 for details).

For the Exposure Photomerge function, all of the photos used have to be of exactly the same shot, otherwise there will be some overlap in the final image.

The Pencil tool is used for several of the Photomerge options. It is used to draw over an area in a source image that is then merged into the final image.

Creating Panoramas

For anyone who takes landscape pictures, sooner or later the desire to create a panorama occurs. With film-based cameras, this usually involves sticking several photographs together to create the panorama, albeit a rather patchwork one. With digital images, the end result can look a lot more professional, and Elements has a dedicated function for achieving this: the Photomerge Panorama.

When creating a panorama there are a few rules to follow:

- If possible, use a tripod to ensure that your camera stays at the same level for all of the shots.

- Keep the same exposure settings for all images.

- Make sure that there is a reasonable overlap between images (about 20%). Some cameras enable you to align the correct overlap between the images.

- Keep the same distance between yourself and the object you are capturing, otherwise the end result will look out of perspective.

To create a panorama:

 In Expert edit mode, open two or more images and select **Guided** > **Photomerge** > **Photomerge Panorama** from the Menu bar

Click on the **Auto Panorama** button to create the panorama automatically from the selected images

Click on the **Create Panorama** button

Beware

Do not include too many images in a panorama, otherwise it could be too large for viewing or printing easily.

Hot tip

Panoramas do not just have to be of landscapes. They can also be used for items such as a row of buildings, or crowds at a sporting event.

Don't forget

In Step 2 there are other options for the style of the panorama.

...cont'd

 The panorama will be created, but with gaps where the images could not be matched. The **Clean Edges** dialog box asks if you would like to fill in the edges of the panorama. Click on the **Yes** button to blend the empty areas with the background

 Panoramas can usually be improved by applying color correction such as Brightness/Contrast and Shadows/Highlights. They can also be cropped to make a narrower panorama to highlight the main subject

5 Artistic Effects

This chapter shows how to create stunning effects and features, to give your photos the "wow" factor. This is done with Guided edit mode where there are numerous templates to follow.

Meme Maker

Memes are graphical images, usually with text added, that are most commonly used for humorous effect on social media. Within the Guided edit mode in Element 2019 it is possible to create your own memes. To do this:

The Meme Maker is a new feature in Elements 2019.

One of the goals of memes is to attract as much attention as possible on social media. However, never put anything rude or offensive in a meme, otherwise you may attract attention for the wrong reasons.

1 Open the image that you want to convert into a meme. Access Guided edit mode and in the **Fun Edits** section, click on the **Meme Maker** button

2 Click on the **Create Meme Template** button to add a border for the meme

3 The meme border is added to the photo (this can be amended in Step 8)

4 Double-click on the pre-inserted text boxes and add the required text for the meme

5 Click on the **Type Tool** button to access the options for formatting the text (drag over the text to select if for formatting)

2. Click the Type Tool button to modify your top and bottom text.

Use the tool options below to adjust the style of your text.

T Type Tool

6 Drag here to resize the photo in the meme, or click on the **Flip** buttons to flip the photo vertically or horizontally

3. Resize your photo to highlight your subject.

Zoom:

Flip:

7 Click on the **Effects** button to add effects to the photo (this is an optional feature)

5. (Optional) Choose an effect for your photo.

ƒx Effects

8 Click on these buttons to add a different border to the meme (this is an optional feature)

4. (Optional) Choose a new border.

9 Click on the **Next** button once all of the editing changes have been made

Next

10 Select what to do with the completed meme. This includes saving it within Elements 2019, editing it within either Quick Edit or Expert Edit mode, or sharing it on a social media site, including Flickr and Twitter

What would you like to do next?

Save:

Save   Save As

Continue Editing:

In Quick   In Expert

Share:

●● Flickr

Twitter

Hot tip

Click on the green check icon to accept text editing changes, or click on the red circle icon to reject them.

Hot tip

Memes created in Elements 2019 can only be shared to a limited range of social media sites from within Elements itself. In order to share them to other sites such as Facebook, click on the **Save As** button in Step 10 and save the image in the JPEG file format. In the Organizer, select the photo and select **Share > Email** from the top toolbar. Email the photo to yourself and then add it to your Facebook page from your smartphone or computer.

Multi-Photo Text

Creating text from a photo is a great way to produce creative messages or posters. In Elements 2019, text effects can be created from multiple photos, not just one. To do this:

Multi-Photo Text is a new feature in Elements 2019.

The text on the background has to be a reasonably large size, so the Multi-Photo Text effect can be seen clearly. Depending on the size of the photo being used for the background, aim to use a text size of 800 points, or higher (the maximum is 1296 points). This can be specified here.

If the **Fit** option is selected in Step 5, the text will be expanded proportionally over the background photo; if **Fill** is selected the text will be expanded, and distorted, to fill the whole area of the photo.

 Open the image that you want to use as the background for the Multi-Photo Text effect

 Access Guided edit mode and in the **Fun Edits** section, click on the **Multi-Photo Text** button

3 Click on the **Type Tool** button to add text to the background photo

> 1. Click the Type Tool button below, and then click your photo and type some text. (Use the tool options along the bottom to adjust the text style.)
>
> **T**   Type Tool

4 Click on the background photo and add the required text. Use the panel below the text to add formatting options

5 Click on these buttons to specify how the text fills the background photo

> 2. (Optional) Choose how you'd like the text to appear on your photo.
>
> Abc   Abc
> Fit   Fill

102

6 Click on the **Create Frames** button to create a frame for each letter

7 Each letter is converted into a frame, into which individual photos can be inserted, and displayed as the shape of each letter

8 Click on a letter to add a photo to it from your computer. Or, click on the **Photo Bin** button to add photos that are currently open in the Photo Bin (photos can be added from your computer from the **Computer** button here too). The selected photos fill the frames in the photo

9 Click on these buttons to add a different background color, or add bevel and shadow effects to the frames (these are optional)

Hot tip

If photos are added from the Photo Bin in Step 8, ensure that there is one more photo in the Photo Bin than the number of letters in the photo: one photo will be used as the background and the rest will be used to fill the frames.

Don't forget

After the options in Step 9, save, edit or share the completed photo, as shown on page 101.

103

Text and Border Overlay

Individual photos can quickly and effectively have both text and a border added to them in Elements 2019. To do this:

Text and Border Overlay is a new feature in Elements 2019.

By default, the text for the text and border overlay effect is placed in the top, left-hand, corner of the border. Click on one of the locations on the border in Step 6 to change the position of the text.

 1 Open the image to which you want to add a text and border overlay effect

 2 Access Guided edit mode and in the **Special Edits** section, click on the **Text and Border Overlay** button

 3 Click on the **Select a Border** button and click on a border style for the photo

4 Click on the **Add Text Overlay** button to create a text box over the photo's border

 5 Click on the **Type Tool** button to add text to the photo. This can be formatted in the options panel

6 Select a position on the border for the text and click on the **Text Styles** button to add a preset style for the text

 7 The text and border are displayed over the photo. Click on the **Next** button to save, edit or share it, as shown on page 101

Painterly Effect

The Painterly effect is one that creates a border around an image to make it look like it has been painted on a canvas. To do this:

 1 Open the image for the Painterly effect

2 Access Guided edit mode and in the **Fun Edits** section, click on the **Painterly** button

3 Click on the **Paint Brush** button and click on the photo to apply the template each time

4 Select a color for the background canvas. Click on the **Select Custom Color** button to select a color other than black or white

5 Select a texture for the background color and an effect for it

6 Click on the **Next** button to complete the Painterly effect and save, edit or share it, as shown on page 101

Texture and Effect are optional for adding to the background.

If a texture is added, the **Opacity** slider can be used to determine how much of the textured background is visible.

shown on page 101

Speed Pan

The Speed Pan effect is a great way to create the effect of motion, and give a photo a dynamic appearance. To do this:

 Open the image to which you want to add the effect of speed

 Access Guided edit mode and in the **Fun Edits** section, click on the **Speed Pan** button

 Click on the **Quick Selection Tool** button and drag it over the part of the image that you want to remain static

 Click on the **Add Motion Blur** button and apply the setting for the amount and direction of motion blur to be added to the background of the image

 Click on the **Refine Effect Brush** button to fine tune the selection against the background

Click on the **Next** button to complete the Speed Pan effect and save, edit or share it, as shown on page 101

106

Frame Creator

Elements 2019 comes with its own range of frames for photos, but you can create your own too. To do this:

1 Open the image that you want to use to create your own photo frame

2 Access Guided edit mode and in the **Special Edits** section, click on the **Frame Creator** button

3 Use one of the selection tools to select an area of the image (this will be used to create the space for a photo to be inserted – the surrounding area will be the frame)

4 Click on the **Create Frame** button

5 Click on the **Save Frame** button

6 Give the frame a name and click on the **OK** button

Enter Frame Name

Please enter a name for your new frame:

Sunset

OK
Cancel

7 Click on the **Done** button to complete the Guided edit and save the frame as a new image (this should be as a PSD image)

Done

Hot tip

To add a photo to your own frame, open the frame file (which has the same name given to the frame in Step 6), open another photo and drag it from the Photo Bin into the frame area.

Beware

Frames that are created with the Frame Creator option are not available from the **Frames** button on the Quick edit mode bottom toolbar. They can be opened as a normal image file (if saved as a PSD file to preserve the layers), and they are also available in Expert edit mode from the **Graphics** panel button (select the **My Frames** option from the **Show All** drop-down menu).

Artistic Overlays

One of the artistic Guided edits can be used to place an artistic shape over a subject in an image and apply effects to the background and within the shape. To do this:

1 Open the image to which you want to add an overlay effect. Access Guided edit mode and in the **Fun Edits** section, click on the **Shape Overlay Effect** button

Add a shape overlay effect to create an artistic look.

2 Click on the **Select a shape** button and click on a shape. The shape is placed over the image

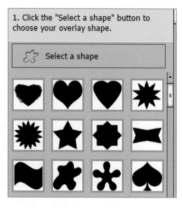

1. Click the "Select a shape" button to choose your overlay shape.

Select a shape

3 Click on the **Move Tool** button and drag the shape into position on the image

Move Tool

Don't forget

Click on the green tick icon to accept the position of the shape once it has been moved using the Move Tool. Click on the red circle to reject it.

Click on the **Outside Effect** button and select an effect for the area outside the selection shape

3. Choose an effect for the area outside of the shape.

⭐ Outside Effect

Don't forget

If you do not like an effect that has been added in Step 4 or 5, click on the Undo button in the panel.

 Click on the **Inside Effect** button and select an effect for the area inside the selection shape

4. Choose an effect for the area inside of the shape.

✴ Inside Effect

6 Click on the **Crop Tool** button to crop the image to a custom size. Click on the **Crop to Shape** button to generate a preset crop

5. (Optional) Crop your photo.

🔲 Crop Tool

Use the Crop Tool to manually crop the photo.

OR

🔲 Crop to Shape

Use Crop to Shape to automatically crop the photo.

109

Hot tip

The **Crop to Shape** option creates a tight crop around the overlay shape. Use the standard **Crop** tool to include more of the background.

7 The **Crop to Shape** option crops the image around the shape that was added in Step 2

8 Click on the **Next** button to complete the overlay effect and save, edit or share it, as shown on page 101

Effects Collage

Individual photos can be quickly and effectively turned into impressive collages in Elements 2019. To do this:

 Open the image that you want to turn into a collage

 Access Guided edit mode and in the **Fun Edits** section, click on the **Effects Collage** button

 Select an option for a layout of the collage; e.g. how the photo is split up

 Select a style for the collage. Click on the down-pointing arrow to access the full range of styles

5 Click on the **Next** button to complete the collage and save, edit or share it, as shown on page 101

110

Hot tip

The option for continuing editing in Expert edit mode (which is accessed on the Save or Share panel as on page 101) is a good way to see the composition of a Guided edit mode image. Click on the **Layers** panel button on the Expert edit mode bottom toolbar to view the layers used to create the image.

6 Beyond Basic Color Editing

This chapter looks at some of the more powerful features for image editing in Elements, so you can take your skills to the next level.

112

By altering the hue of an image, some interesting abstract color effects can be created. This can be very effective if you are producing several versions of the same image, such as for an artistic poster.

Hue is used to describe the color of a particular pixel or an image.

Hue and Saturation

The Hue/Saturation command can be used to edit the color elements of an image. However, it works slightly differently from other commands, such as those for the brightness and contrast. There are three areas that are covered by the Hue/Saturation command: color (hue), color strength (saturation) and lightness. To adjust the hue and saturation of an image:

 Open an image

 Select **Enhance > Adjust Color > Adjust Hue/ Saturation** from the Menu bar, in either Expert or Quick edit modes

 Drag this slider to adjust the hue of the image; i.e. change the colors in the image

4   Drag this slider to adjust the saturation; i.e. the intensity of colors in the image

The Lightness option is similar to adjusting image brightness.

5   Check on the **Colorize** box to color the image with the hue of the currently-selected foreground color in the Color Picker, which is located at the bottom of the Toolbox

The Colorize option can be used to create some interesting "color wash" effects. Try altering the Hue slider once the Colorize box has been checked On.

113

6   Click on the **OK** button to apply any changes that have been made

For more on working with color and the Color Picker, see page 164.

Histogram

The Histogram in Elements is a device that displays the tonal range of the pixels in an image, and it can be used for very precise editing of an image. The Histogram (**Window** > **Histogram** in Expert edit mode) is a graph that displays how the pixels in an image are distributed across the image, from the darkest (black) to the lightest (white) points. Another way of considering the Histogram is that it displays the values of an image's highlights, midtones and shadows:

The keyboard shortcut for accessing the Histogram is F9.

The Histogram works by looking at the individual color channels of an image (Red, Green, Blue, also known as the RGB color model) or a combination of all three, which is displayed as Luminosity in the Channel box. It can also look at all of the colors in an image.

114

Image formats such as JPEG are edited in Elements using the RGB color model; i.e. red, green and blue, mixed together to create the colors in the image.

Ideally, the Histogram should show a reasonably consistent range of tonal distribution, indicating an image that has good contrast and detail:

Click here to select specific color channels to view in the Histogram.

However, if the tonal range is bunched at one end of the graph, this indicates that the image is under-exposed or over-exposed:

Over-exposure

If the Histogram is left open, it will update automatically as editing changes are made to an image. This gives a good idea of how effective the changes are.

Under-exposure

Levels

While the Histogram displays the tonal range of an image, the Levels function can be used to edit this range. Any changes made using the Levels function will then be visible in the Histogram. Levels allows you to redistribute pixels between the darkest and lightest points in an image, and also set these points manually if you want to. To use the Levels function:

Hot tip

The Levels function can be used to adjust the tonal range of a specific area of an image, by first making a selection and then using the Levels dialog box. For more details on selecting areas, see Chapter 7.

Don't forget

In the Levels dialog box, the graph is the same as the one shown in the Histogram.

Don't forget

Image shadows, midtones and highlights can be altered by dragging the markers for the black, midtone and white input points.

  Open an image

  Select **Enhance** > **Adjust Lighting** > **Levels** from the Menu bar, in either Expert or Quick edit modes

Midtone input point

Black input point

White input point

Output points

3 Drag the black point and the white point sliders to, or beyond, the first pixels denoted in the graph to increase the contrast

It is worth adjusting an image's black and white points before any other editing is performed.

Move the midtone point slider to darken or lighten the midtones in an image.

4 Drag the output sliders towards the middle to decrease the contrast

The Auto button in the Levels dialog box produces the same effect as using the **Enhance** > **Auto Levels** command from the Menu bar.

117

Adjustments with Levels

Although there is an Auto Levels function within Elements, more accurate editing can be done by using the Levels dialog box:

The Auto Levels option can be accessed by selecting **Enhance** > **Auto Levels** from the Menu bar.

The keyboard shortcut for accessing the Levels dialog window is Ctrl + L (Command key + L on a Mac).

By default, all of the color channels (RGB for Red, Green and Blue) are edited within Levels. However, click here to select the individual Red, Green and Blue channels so that they can be edited independently.

1 Open an image that is either too dark or too light (or requires the midtones to be edited)

2 Select **Enhance** > **Adjust Lighting** > **Levels** from the Menu bar

3 If there is no data at one end of the graph, it suggests an image is either too dark or too light (in this instance, too dark). Drag on this button to adjust the image

...cont'd

...cont'd

4 Drag the button to where the graph starts (or finishes). Ideally, the white and black buttons should be at the right and left of the graph respectively

Input Levels:

0 1.00 191

5 Drag on this button to adjust the midtones of an image; i.e. the color in the mid-range between white and black

6 The Levels editing effects are applied to the image

7 Click on the **OK** button to exit the Levels dialog window

OK

Hot tip

Adjusting the midtones manually is similar to using **Enhance** > **Adjust Lighting** > **Shadows/Highlights** from the Menu bar.

Don't forget

Levels can also be accessed and applied in Quick edit mode.

Color Curves

If the colors are not ideal in a photo, one option for editing them is with Color Curves. This is done by editing the colors for different elements in the image; e.g. highlights, brightness, contrast and shadows. This can be done with preset options, or you can apply your own settings manually. To use Color Curves:

There is no keyboard shortcut for accessing the Color Curves dialog window.

Color Curves edits the color using the overall color channels in an image. These are the individual Red, Green or Blue channels, or a combination of all three: the RGB channel.

1 Select **Enhance** > **Adjust Color** > **Adjust Color Curves** from the Menu bar. The Adjust Color Curves window has a **Before** and **After** preview panel at the top of the window, and options for automatic and manual adjustments at the bottom of the window

2 Under the **Select a Style:** heading, select the area of color that you want to edit. These include **Backlight** (for images where the foreground subject is too dark), **Darken Highlights**, **Default**, **Increase Contrast**, **Increase Midtones**, **Lighten Shadows** and **Solarize**

To avoid photos where the foreground subject is too dark, use the flash when taking a photo, even when there is bright sunlight behind the subject.

120

For each item selected in Step 2, the appropriate curve adjustments are made automatically (shown on the graph)

 Drag the sliders under **Adjust Sliders:** to edit the color elements in the image manually. As you drag the sliders, the graph moves accordingly

Hot tip

Dragging the sliders in Step 4 is a good way to see how the shape of the Color Curves graph affects the image.

Before   After

 Click on the **OK** button to apply the changes, **Cancel** to remove them, or **Reset** to return to the original image and continue editing it

Hot tip

Exaggerated colors created with curves can make a striking photo, even if it is not completely realistic.

Remove Color Cast

Even sophisticated digital cameras and smartphone cameras can sometimes misinterpret the lighting conditions of a scene, resulting in an unnatural color in the photo, known as color cast. To remove this:

Don't forget

There is no keyboard shortcut for accessing the Remove Color Cast dialog window.

Don't forget

Color cast is particularly common in indoor shots taken without the flash under artificial lighting. This is known as "white balance", where the camera does not correctly interpret what white should be, and so all of the other colors in the photo are affected too. One way to overcome this is to change your camera's white balance settings if you are taking photos in artificial lighting.

Hot tip

Color cast can be edited manually within Levels. To do this, select one of the individual color channels (Red, Green or Blue) in the Levels dialog window and drag the input sliders accordingly.

 In Expert or Quick edit modes, open the photo affected by color cast

Select **Enhance > Adjust Color > Remove Color Cast** from the Menu bar. Click on an area of the photo that should be black, white or gray. The overall color in the photo will be adjusted accordingly

7

Working with Selections

The true power of digital image editing comes into its own when you are able to select areas of an image and edit them independently. This chapter looks at the various ways that selections can be made and edited, using the tools and functions within Elements.

About Selections

One of the most important aspects of image editing is the ability to select areas within an image. This can be used in a number of different ways:

- Selecting an object to apply an editing technique to it (such as changing the brightness or contrast) without affecting the rest of the image.

- Selecting a particular color in an image.

- Selecting an area on which to apply a special effect.

- Selecting an area to remove.

Expert edit mode has several tools that can be used to select items, and there are also a number of editing functions that can be applied to selections.

Two examples of how selections can be used are:

Don't forget

Once a selection has been made, it stays selected even when another tool is activated, to allow further editing to take place.

Don't forget

If a selection is deleted, the space will be filled by the current background color in the Color Picker in the Toolbox.

Hot tip

The best way to deselect a selection is to click on it once with one of the selection tools, preferably the one used to make the selection. You can also choose **Select** > **Deselect** from the Menu bar.

 Select an area within an image and delete it

 Select an area in an image and add a color or special effect

Marquee Tools

There are two options for the Marquee tool: the Rectangular Marquee tool and the Elliptical Marquee tool. Both of these can be used to make symmetrical selections. To use the Marquee tools:

1 Select either the **Rectangular** or the **Elliptical Marquee** tool from the Toolbox. Select the required options from the Tool Options bar

2 Make a symmetrical selection with one of the tools by clicking and dragging on an image

To access additional tools from the Expert edit mode Toolbox, click on a tool and select any grouped tools in the Tool Options bar.

Elliptical selection

Rectangular selection

To make a selection that is exactly square or round, hold down **Shift** when dragging with the Rectangular Marquee tool or the Elliptical Marquee tool respectively.

Lasso Tools

There are three options for the Lasso tool, which can be used to make freehand selections. To use these:

Lasso tool

1 Select the **Lasso** tool from the Toolbox and select the required options from the Tool Options bar

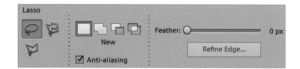

2 Make a freehand selection by clicking with the mouse and dragging around the object

Polygonal Lasso tool

1 Select the **Polygonal Lasso** tool from the Toolbox and select the required options from the Tool Options bar

2 Make a selection by clicking on specific points around an object, and then dragging to the next point

Hot tip

When a selection has been completed (i.e. its end point reaches its start point), a small circle will appear at the side of whichever Lasso tool is being used. Click on this point to complete the selection.

Don't forget

See page 150 for information about Anti-aliasing, which can be accessed in the Tool Options bar.

Beware

With the Lasso tool, do not release the mouse until the selection has been completed.

Don't forget

Making a selection with the Polygonal Lasso tool is like creating a dot-to-dot pattern.

Magnetic Lasso tool

1 Select the **Magnetic Lasso** tool from the Toolbox and select the required options from the Tool Options bar

2 Click once on an image to create the first anchor point

In the Tool Options bar for the Magnetic Lasso tool, the Contrast value determines the amount of contrast there has to be between colors for the selection line to snap to them. A high value detects lines with a high contrast, and vice versa.

127

3 Make a selection by dragging continuously around an object. The selection line snaps to the closest, strongest edge; i.e. the one with the most contrast. Fastening points are added as the selection is made

The Frequency setting in the Tool Options bar determines how quickly the fastening points are inserted as a selection is being made. A high value places the fastening points more quickly than a low value.

Magic Wand Tool

The Magic Wand tool can be used to select areas of the same or similar color. To do this:

Don't forget

In the Tool Options bar for the Magic Wand tool, the Tolerance box determines the range of colors that will be selected in relation to the color you click on. A low value will only select a very narrow range of colors in relation to the initially-selected one, while a high value will include a greater range. The values range from 0-255.

1 Select the **Magic Wand** tool from the Toolbox and select the required options from the Tool Options bar

2 Click on a color to select all of the adjacent pixels that are the same or similar color, depending on the options selected from the Tool Options bar

Hot tip

In the Tool Options bar for the Magic Wand tool, check on the **Contiguous** box to ensure that only adjacent colors are selected. To select the same or similar color throughout the image, whether adjacent or not, uncheck the Contiguous box.

128

Selection Brush Tool

The Selection Brush tool can be used to select areas by using a brush-like stroke. Unlike with the Marquee or Lasso tools, the area selected by the Selection Brush tool is the one directly below where the tool moves. To make a selection with the Selection Brush tool (this is also available in Quick edit mode):

 1 Select the **Selection Brush** tool from the Toolbox and select the required options from the Tool Options bar

 2 Click and drag to make a selection

 3 The selection area is within the borders marked out by the Selection Brush tool

Quick Selection Tool

The Quick Selection tool can be used to select areas of similar color by drawing over the general area, without having to make a specific selection. To do this:

 Select the **Quick Selection** tool from the Toolbox

 Select the required options from the Tool Options bar

Draw over an area, or part of an area, to select all of the similarly-colored pixels

Don't forget

The Quick Selection tool is also available from the Quick edit mode Toolbox.

Beware

If a very large brush size is used for the Quick Selection tool – e.g. 300 px (pixels) or above – you may select unwanted areas of the image by mistake.

Don't forget

As you drag the Quick Selection tool, it selects whichever areas of color it passes over. As you drag over different areas of color, these will be selected too.

Smart Brush Tool

The Smart Brush tool can be used to quickly select large areas in an image (in a similar way to the Quick Selection tool) and then have effects applied automatically to the selected area. To do this:

 Open the image to which you want to apply changes

 Select the **Smart Brush** tool from the Toolbox

 Select the editing effect you want to apply to the area selected by the Smart Brush tool, from the Tool Options bar

Select **Brush size** for the Smart Brush tool, from the Tool Options bar

Drag the Smart Brush tool over an area of the image. In the left-hand image below, the building has been selected and brightened; in the right-hand image, the sky has been selected and enhanced

Multiple editing effects can be applied with the Smart Brush tool within the same image. This usually requires individually selecting different parts of the image and then selecting the required effect.

Some of the other options for the Smart Brush tool include increasing the brightness or contrast, intensifying foliage in a photo, making lips redder, and creating sepia images.

Auto Selections

Instead of having to make precise selections, Elements 2019 has a function where selections can be made by dragging around a subject. Elements can then identify the subject and select it.

Once a selection has been made, it can be inverted by choosing **Select** > **Inverse** from the Menu bar. The keyboard shortcut for inverting a selection is Shift + Ctrl + I (Shift + Command key + I on a Mac).

 Open an image and select the **Auto Selection** tool (from the selection tools subset)

 Drag the **Auto Selection** tool around the required subject. This creates a rectangular box

When a selection has been inverted, the newly-selected area can be edited in the same way as for a standard selection in a photo.

 Release the **Auto Selection** tool to enable it to create the selection

Once a selection has been made in this way it can be edited independently from the rest of the image. Also, if the selection is inverted (see tip) the background can be edited and the originally-selected subject remains untouched

Feathering

Feathering is a technique that can be used to soften the edges of a selection by making them slightly blurry. This can be used if you are pasting a selection into another image, or if you want to soften the edges around a portrait of an individual. To do this:

  Make a selection

2 Choose **Select** > **Feather** from the Menu bar

The keyboard shortcut for accessing the Feather Selection dialog window is Alt + Ctrl + D (Alt + Command key + D on a Mac).

3 Enter a Feather Radius value (the number of pixels wide around the radius of the selection that will be blurred). Click on the **OK** button

Feather Selection ✕
❓ **Learn more about:** Feather Selection   OK   Cancel
Feather Radius: 5   pixels

Feathering can also be selected from the Tool Options bar once a Marquee tool is selected, and before the selection has been made.

4 Invert the selection, as shown on the previous page, and delete the background by pressing **Delete** on the keyboard. This will leave the selection around the subject with softened edges

If required, crop the final image so that the feathered subject is more prominent.

Refining Selections

When making selections it is sometimes difficult to exactly select the area that you want. In Elements 2019 it is possible to refine the area of a selection, and also the edges around a selected item. To do this:

The **Refine Selection Brush** option can be used regardless of how the selection was made.

Click inside a selection to add to it; click outside to subtract from it.

Click on the **View** box to select an option for the overlay that covers the current selection, so that you can see exactly what has been selected.

 In Expert or Quick edit mode, make a selection with one of the selection tools

 Select the **Refine Selection Brush** tool (grouped with the Quick Selection tool)

 Click on this button to add or subtract from the selection with the cursor

4 Click on this button to smooth the edges of the selection by dragging the cursor over it

5 Select a size for the cursor to refine the selection, and the strength for how it snaps to neighboring pixels; the greater the strength, the more the selection will snap to pixels of similar color

134

6 Position the cursor inside or outside the selection. It appears as two circles: a smaller one inside a larger one. Use the circles to nudge the selection lines one way or another to refine the selection

Zoom in on a selection for the greatest accuracy in refining it.

Refining edges

It is also possible to add a range of refinements to the edges of a selection, which can be an excellent option for textures such as clothing or animal fur. To do this:

1 Once a selection has been made, click on the **Refine Edge...** button in the Tool Options bar

Refine Edge...

2 Select options here for how much of the edge is detected in terms of being refined. Select **Smart Radius** or enter a manual value for the radius

3 Select options here for how the edge is adjusted, using smoothing, feathering, contrast and moving the edge. Click **OK**

The Refine Edge options are particularly useful if you are copying a selection and pasting it into another image that has different textures.

Once an area has been moved and deselected, it cannot then be selected independently again, unless it has been copied and pasted onto a separate layer.

Selections can also be deselected by clicking on **Select** > **Deselect** from the Menu bar, or using Ctrl + D on the keyboard (Command key + D on a Mac).

Editing Selections

When you have made a selection you can edit it in a number of ways:

Moving a selection

Make a selection and select the **Move** tool from the Toolbox. Drag the selection to move it to a new location.

Changing the selection area

Make a selection with a selection tool. With the same tool selected, click and drag within the selection area to move it over another part of the image.

Adding to a selection

Make a selection and click on this button in the Tool Options bar. Make another selection to create a single, larger selection. The two selections do not have to intersect.

Intersecting with a selection

To create a selection by intersecting two existing selections, make a selection and click on this button in the Tool Options bar. Make another selection that intersects the first. The intersected area will become the selection.

Expanding a selection

To expand a selection by a specific number of pixels, make a selection and choose **Select** > **Modify** > **Expand** from the Menu bar. In the **Expand Selection** dialog box, enter the amount by which you want the selection expanded.

Growing a selection

The Grow command can be used on a selection when it has been made with the Magic Wand tool, and some of the pixels within the selection have been omitted. To do this:

 Make a selection with the **Magic Wand** tool and make the required choices from the Tool Options bar

 Choose **Select** > **Grow** from the Menu bar

Depending on the choices in the Tool Options bar, the omitted pixels will be included in the selection.

8 Layers

Layers provide the means to add numerous elements to an image, and edit them independently from one another. This chapter looks at how to use layers to add content to photos.

Layering Images

Layering is a technique that enables you to add additional elements to an image, and place them on separate layers so that they can be edited and manipulated independently from other elements in the image. It is like creating an image using transparent sheets of film: each layer is independent of the others, but when they are combined, a composite image is created. This is an extremely versatile technique for working with digital images.

By using layers, several different elements can be combined to create a composite image:

Original image

Final image
With text, gradient and shapes added (four additional layers have been added).

Layers should usually be used when you are adding content to an image, as this gives more flexibility for working with the various image elements once they have been added.

Text and shapes cannot be added together on the same layer.

Layers Panel

The use of layers within Elements is done within Expert edit mode and is governed by the Layers panel. When an image is first opened it is shown in the Layers panel as the Background layer. While this remains as the Background layer, it cannot be moved above any other layers. However, it can be converted into a normal layer, in which case it operates in the same way as any other layer. To convert a Background layer into a normal one:

The keyboard shortcut for accessing the Layers panel is F11.

1 Click on the **Layers** button on the Taskbar

2 The open image is shown in the Layers panel as the Background

The Background layer can also be converted into a normal one by applying the Background Eraser tool and the Magic Eraser tool.

3 Double-click on the layer. Enter a name for it and click on the **OK** button

New Layer	✕
Name: Bridges	OK
☐ Use Previous Layer to Create Clipping Mask	Cancel
Mode: Normal ▼ Opacity: 100 ▼ %	

The Layers panel menu can be accessed from the button in the top right-hand corner of the Layers panel.

4 The Background layer is converted into a normal layer in the Layers panel

Adding Layers

New blank layers can be added whenever you want to include new content within an image. This could be part of another image that has been copied and pasted; a whole new image; some text; or an object. To add a new layer:

Hot tip

The keyboard shortcut for adding a new layer is Shift + Ctrl + N (Shift + Command key + N on a Mac).

1 Click here on the Layers panel

Don't forget

Text is automatically added on a new layer within an image.

2 Double-click on the layer name and overtype to give the layer a new name

Don't forget

To edit an item on a particular layer, first make sure that the correct layer is selected in the Layers panel. A selected layer is known as the active layer and it is highlighted in the Layers panel with a solid color around it.

3 With the new layer selected in the Layers panel, add content to this layer. This will be visible over the layer, or layers, below it

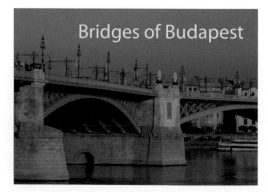

Fill and Adjustment Layers

Fill and Adjustment layers can be added to images to give an effect behind or above the main subject. To do this:

1 Open the Layers panel and select a layer. The Fill or Adjustment layer will be placed directly above the selected layer

2 Click here at the bottom of the Layers panel

3 Select one of the Fill or Adjustment options. The Fill options are **Solid Color...**, **Gradient...** or **Pattern...**

Solid Color...
Gradient...
Pattern...

Levels...
Brightness/Contrast...

Hue/Saturation...
Gradient Map...
Photo Filter...

Invert
Threshold...
Posterize...

...cont'd

Fill and Adjustment layers can also be added from the Layer option on the Menu bar.

If you want to edit a Fill or Adjustment layer, double-click on its icon in the Layers panel and then apply the required changes.

142

If the opacity for a Fill layer is 100%, nothing will be visible beneath that layer.

4 For a Solid Color, Gradient or Pattern Fill, the required Fill is selected from the dialog box and this is added to the selected layer

5 For Adjustment options, settings can be applied within the Adjustments panel

6 Once Fill and Adjustment settings have been applied, the effect can be edited by changing the opacity. This is done by dragging this slider, which appears when the Opacity box is clicked On

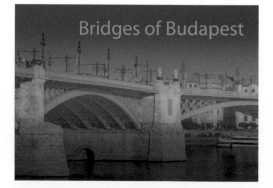

7 The opacity level determines how much of the image is visible through the Fill or Adjustment layer

Bridges of Budapest

Working with Layers

Moving layers

The order in which layers are arranged in the Layers panel is known as the stacking order. It is possible to change a layer's position in the stacking order, which affects how it is viewed in the composite image. To do this:

1 Click and drag a layer within the Layers panel to change its stacking order

Layers cannot be moved underneath the Background layer, unless it has been renamed.

Hiding layers

Layers can be hidden while you are working on other parts of an image. However, the layer is still part of the composite image – it has not been removed. To hide a layer:

1 Click here so that a line appears through the eye icon, and the layer becomes hidden. Click again to remove the line and reveal the layer

This icon indicates that the layer has a layer mask linked to it. This means that the mask will move with the layer, if it is moved. Click on the icon to unlink the layer mask from the layer (see pages 144-146 for details about layer masks).

143

Locking layers

Layers can be locked, so that they cannot be edited accidentally while you are working on other parts of an image. To do this:

1 Select a layer and click here so that the padlock is activated. The padlock also appears on the layer itself

Layers can be deleted by selecting them and clicking on the **Trash** icon in the Layers panel. However, this also deletes all of the content on that layer.

Layer Masks

Because layers can be separated within an individual image, there is a certain amount of versatility in terms of the ways in which different layers can interact with each other. One of these ways is to create a Layer Mask. This is a top-level layer, through which an area is removed so that the layer below is revealed. To do this:

Beware

If the Background layer is not renamed as in Step 2, the graphic will be placed directly over the Background layer, rather than being created on a new layer.

Don't forget

When creating the new layer in Step 2, you can also change the opacity and select a different mode, to affect the way the layer interacts with layers below it (if there are any).

Don't forget

Different types of content can be added as the top layer in an image to be used as a Layer Mask, although whatever is added has to be converted to a normal layer rather than a background one.

1 Open an image. It will be displayed as the Background in the Layers panel. Double-click on this to select it

2 Give the layer a new name and click on the **OK** button

3 Click on the **Graphics** button on the Taskbar to access the Graphics panel

4 Use the drop-down menus at the top of the Graphics panel to access different categories and click on a graphic to select it

5 Select a graphic and double-click on it to add it as a layer to the current image. Initially, this is added below the open image. Rename the new layer

Don't forget

If a new layer is not renamed, it will automatically become the Background one.

6 Drag the added layer above the original image (this can also be done by selecting an area in another image, copying it and then pasting it above the existing image)

Beware

The top layer will obscure all layers below it, until either its opacity is reduced, or a Layer Mask is applied.

7 The graphic image layer now covers the original one

Hot tip

If numerous layers are used within a single image they can be grouped together within the Layers panel. Select layers within the panel and drag them over this button to create a group of layers that can be managed and edited as a single entity:

145

...cont'd

If the Brush tool is used to create the Layer Mask, this is done by drawing over the top layer of the image. As this is done, the layer below will be revealed. Change the level of opacity in the Tool Options bar to change the amount that the layer below shows through the top layer of the image.

The selected layer can also be deleted by pressing the **Delete** key on the keyboard.

Build up an image with several Layer Masks, to create an artistic effect.

 Click here to apply a layer mask to the top layer

 Select either one of the **Marquee** tools, the **Lasso** tools, or the **Brush** tool from the Toolbox

 Select an area on the top layer and delete it, to display the image below it (**Edit** > **Delete** from the Menu bar)

In the Layers panel, the area that has been removed is displayed here

Opacity

The opacity of a layer can be set to determine how much of the layer below is visible through the selected layer. To do this:

1 Select a layer either in the Layers panel or by clicking on the relevant item within an image

2 Click here and drag the slider that appears below, to achieve the required level of opacity. The greater the amount of opacity, the less transparent the selected layer becomes

3 The opacity setting determines how much of the background or the layer below is visible through the selected one. This can be used to create some interesting artistic effects, including a watermark effect if the opacity is applied to a single layer with nothing behind it

Hot tip

The background behind an image to which opacity has been applied can be changed within the Preferences section. Select **Edit > Preferences** from the Menu bar (**Adobe Photoshop Elements Editor > Preferences** on a Mac) and then select **Transparency** and edit the items in the Grid Colors box.

Don't forget

Different layers can have different levels of opacity applied to them.

Saving Layers

Once an image has been created using two or more layers, there are two ways in which the composite image can be saved: in a proprietary Photoshop format, in which case individual layers are maintained; or in a general file format, where all of the layers will be merged into a single one. The advantage of the former is that individual elements can still be edited within the image, independently of other items. In general, it is good practice to save layered images in both a Photoshop and a non-Photoshop format. To save layered images in a Photoshop format:

Before a layer is saved, it is possible to create a composite image consisting of a single layer. To do this, select **Layer** > **Flatten Image** from the Menu bar. To merge the existing layer and the one below it, select **Layer** > **Merge Down** from the Menu bar, and to merge all visible content (excluding any layers that have been hidden) select **Layer** > **Merge Visible**. If layers are flattened, they cannot then be edited independently.

1 Select **File** > **Save As** from the Menu bar

2 Make sure Photoshop (*.PSD, *.PDD) is selected as the format

3 Make sure the Layers box is checked On

4 Click on the **Save** button

Layered images that are saved in the Photoshop PSD/PDD format can increase dramatically in file size, compared with the original image or a layered image that has been flattened.

To save in a non-Photoshop format, select **File** > **Save As** from the Menu bar. Select the file format from the Format box (such as JPEG or TIFF) and click on the **Save** button. The Layers box will not be available.

148

9 Text and Drawing Tools

Elements has options for adding and formatting text, and creating a variety of graphical objects. This chapter looks at how to add and manipulate text and drawing objects.

Adding and Formatting Text

Text can be added to images in Elements and this can be used to create a wide range of items such as cards, brochures and posters. To add text to an image:

Use the Vertical Type tool sparingly, as this is not a natural way for the eye to read text. Use it with small amounts of text, for effect.

150

 1 Select the **Horizontal** or **Vertical Type** tool from the Toolbox

2 Drag on the image with the Type tool to create a text box

3 Make the required formatting selections from the Tool Options bar:

Don't forget

Anti-aliasing is a technique that smoothes out the jagged edges that can sometimes appear with text when viewed on a computer monitor. Anti-aliasing is created by adding pixels to the edges of text, so that it blends more smoothly with the background.

Type tools   Font type   Font size   Color

Type ◢ Horizontal

Myriad Pro Light Condensed   ▼   Color: ▮▼

Light Conden... ▼   Size: 72 pt ▼

Leading: (Auto) ▼   Tracking: 0 ▼

Font style   Spacing

Bold, Italics and Underline

B *I* U S

T↓ T   Warped text

☑ Anti-aliasing

Alignment   Anti-aliasing

4 Type the text onto the image. This is automatically placed onto the image as a new layer, at the top of the stacking order in the Layers panel

Each new text box is placed on a new layer.

5 To move the text, select it with the **Move** tool, then click and drag it to a new position

If there are two or more text layers, they can be moved above or below each other in the Layers panel.

To format text that has already been entered:

Individual words can be selected by double-clicking on them. Text blocks without any returns in the text can be selected by triple-clicking on them. Text blocks containing returns in the text can be selected by quadruple-clicking on them.

1 Select a **Type** tool and drag it over a piece of text to select it

2 Make the changes in the Tool Options bar, as shown in Step 3 on the previous page

3 Click on the green check mark to accept the text entry

Customizing Text

As well as adding standard text, it is also possible to add text to follow a selection, a shape or a custom path. This can be done within Expert edit and Quick edit modes.

Adding text to a selection

To add text to a selection within an image:

In Expert edit mode, select the Move tool and click and drag the text to move it with the selection area.

1 Click on the **Type** tool and select the **Text on Selection** tool option

2 Drag over an area of an image to make a selection

3 Click on the green check mark to accept the selection

4 Click anywhere on the selection and add text. By default, this will be displayed along the outside of the selection

Text on Selection text should be reasonably large in size, so that it can be read clearly on the image.

5 Format the text in the same way as with standard text

152

Adding text to a shape
To add text to a shape within an image:

 Click on the **Type** tool and select the **Text on Shape** tool option

Beware

The butterfly shape is an artistic one, but it can be difficult reading text that is added in this way.

 Click here in the Tool Options bar to select a shape

 Drag over an area of an image to create a shape

 Hot tip

Once customized text has been added and accepted, it can still be edited in the same way as standard text, by using the Horizontal Type Tool and selecting the customized text.

 Click anywhere on the shape and add text. Click on the green check mark as in Step 3 on the previous page

Format the text in the same way as with standard text

 Beware

Make sure that there is a good contrast between the text color and the background colors in the image.

...cont'd

Adding text to a custom path

Text can also be added to a custom path that you draw onto an image. To do this:

Don't forget

The Modify button in Step 2 is used to edit an existing text path. See the next page for more information.

Hot tip

If there are natural contours in an image, these can be used for the custom path.

Don't forget

More than one text path can be added to an image, if required.

1 Open the image onto which you want to create text on a custom path

2 Click on the **Type** tool and select the **Text on Path** tool option. Make sure the **Draw** button is also selected

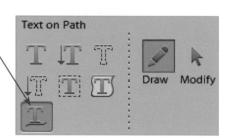

3 Draw a custom path on the image

4 Click on the green check mark to accept the text path

5 Click anywhere on the custom path and add text

Always check the spelling when adding text to a custom path, or any other text in an image.

6 Format the text in the same way as with standard text

Double-click on the text on a text path to select it and edit it, if required.

7 Click on the **Modify** tool in the Tool Options bar. This activates the markers along the custom path

8 Drag the markers to move the position of the custom path

If there is too much text on a custom path it can become jumbled, particularly if you adjust the markers on the path.

9 The custom path can be used to position text in a variety of ways around objects or people

Distorting Text

In addition to producing standard text, it is also possible to create some dramatic effects by distorting text. To do this:

 Enter plain text and select it by dragging a **Type** tool over it

 Click the **Create Warped Text** button on the Tool Options bar

 Click here and select one of the options in the Warp Text dialog box. Click on the **OK** button

4 The selected effect is applied to the text

Text and Shape Masks

Text Masks can be used to reveal an area of an image showing through the text. This can be used to produce eye-catching headings and slogans. To do this:

 Select the **Horizontal** or **Vertical Type Mask** tool from the Toolbox

 Click on an image, then enter and format text as you would for normal text. A red mask is applied to the image when the mask text is entered

 Press **Enter** or click the **Move** tool to border the mask text with dots

Text Mask effects work best if the text used is fairly large in size. In some cases it is a good idea to use bold text, as this is wider than standard text.

Text and Shape Masks are always red and do not show in the final image.

A range of shapes can be added to an image from the Custom Shape tool in the Toolbox.

Text Masks can also be moved around in the original image, using the **Move** tool.

 Select **Edit** > **Copy** from the Menu bar

 Select **File** > **New** from the Menu bar and create a new file

 Select **Edit** > **Paste** from the Menu bar to paste the Text Mask into the new file

Once a Text Mask has been copied, it can also be pasted into other types of documents such as Word and desktop publishing documents.

Cookie Cutter masks

A similar effect can be created with Shape Masks by using the Cookie Cutter tool (grouped with the Crop tool):

 Select the **Cookie Cutter** tool in the Toolbox and click here to select a particular style in the Tool Options bar

The Cookie Cutter shapes have several different categories that can be selected from the **Shapes** box above the current shapes. The categories include: Animals, Flowers, Music, Nature, Ornaments, Signs, and Talk Bubbles.

Drag on an image to create a cut-out effect

Paint Bucket Tool

The Paint Bucket tool can be used to add a solid color to a selection or an area in an image. To do this:

1 Open the image to which you want to apply the solid color using the Paint Bucket tool

For more information on working with color, see page 164.

2 Select the **Paint Bucket** tool from the Toolbox (the foreground color is selected by default)

The Paint Bucket tool can also be loaded with a pattern.

3 Select the **Opacity** and **Tolerance** in the Tool Options bar. The Tolerance determines how much of an image is affected by the Paint Bucket

The higher the tolerance, the greater the area of color applied with the Paint Bucket tool.

4 Click once on an area of solid color with the Paint Bucket tool. The color specified in Step 2 will be applied

Make a selection on an image and then apply the Paint Bucket tool to it, to get the color added exactly where you want.

Gradient Tool

The Gradient tool can be used to add a Gradient Fill to a selection in an image, or to an entire image. To do this:

Beware

If no selection is made for a Gradient Fill, the effect will be applied to the entire selected layer.

Hot tip

The default Gradient effect in the Tool Options bar is created with the currently-selected foreground and background colors within the Toolbox.

 Select an area in an image or select an object

 Select the **Gradient** tool from the Toolbox

 Click here in the Tool Options bar to select preset Gradient Fills

4 Click on a Gradient style to apply it as the default

5 Click here in the Tool Options bar to access the **Gradient Editor** dialog box

To create a new preset Gradient, create it in the Gradient Editor dialog box and click on the **Add to Preset** button, to add it to the list of preset Gradients. Click on the Gradient's icon to give it a unique name in the **Name** box.

 6 Click and drag the sliders to change the amount of a particular color in the Gradient

The more color markers that are added in Step 7, the more complex the final Gradient will be.

7 Click along here to add a new color marker. Click on the **OK** button

 8 Click an icon in the Tool Options bar to select a Gradient style

Radial

9 Click and drag within the original selection to specify the start and end points of the Gradient effect

The amount that the cursor is dragged when adding a Gradient determines where the centerpoint of the Gradient is located, and also the size of each segment of the Gradient.

Brush Tool Settings

The Brush tool is very versatile and can be used to create lines of varying thickness and style. There are numerous settings that can be applied, for different styles and effects. To use this:

1 Select the **Brush** tool from the Toolbox. The options are shown in the Tool Options bar

2 Click here to select a default brush style

3 Select a brush size and style (Hard or Rounded edges) or scroll through the **Brush** box to select different brush styles

4 Click here to select a different brush type

162

5 Select a size and style for the brush selected in Step 4

Hot tip

Brush size can also be altered for custom brush styles created with the Define Brush command (see the first Hot tip on the previous page).

6 Click on the **Brush Settings...** button in Step 2 to make selections for the appearance of the brush

Brush Settings...

7 Drag these sliders to apply the settings for each brush type

Hot tip

Experiment with small changes initially in Step 7, to get an idea of what each effect looks like. Then build up the effect with a greater percentage, if required.

Here are some examples:

- From top to bottom: default brushes with hard edges, rounded edges and 50% opacity applied.

- From top to bottom: default brushes with **Scatter** applied at 50% and **Hue Jitter** at 50%.

Beware

Do not use too many different brush styles on a single image, as it could become a bit overpowering in terms of design.

- From top to bottom: the **Calligraphic Brush** and the **Special Effects Brush (Drippy Watercolor)**.

Always check the foreground and background colors before you add any colors to an image, to ensure you have the right ones.

Whenever the foreground or background color squares are clicked on, the Color Picker tool is automatically activated. This can be used to select a color from anywhere on the screen.

The Color Swatches panel can be used to access different color panels that can be used to select the foreground and background colors. To do this: select **Window** > **Color Swatches** from the Menu bar and click on a color to select it.

Working with Color

All of the text and drawing tools make extensive use of color. Elements provides a number of methods for selecting colors, and also for working with them.

Foreground and background colors

At the bottom of the Toolbox there are two colored squares. These represent the currently-selected foreground and background colors. The foreground color, which is the most frequently used, is the one that is applied to drawing objects, such as fills and lines, and also text. The background color is used for items such as Gradient Fills, and for areas that have been removed with the Eraser tool.

Foreground color   Swap foreground and background colors

Set foreground to black and background to white

Background color

Color Picker

The Color Picker can be used to select a new color for the foreground or background color. To do this:

1 Click once on the foreground or the background color square, as required

2 In the Color Picker, click to select a color

3 Click on the **OK** button

10 Becoming an Elements Expert

This chapter looks at some of the more advanced areas of Elements. These include working with the RAW file format, editing groups of images, creating catalogs and resizing images.

Importing RAW Images

RAW images are those in which the digital data has not been processed in any way, or converted into any specific file format by the camera when they were captured. These produce high quality images and are usually available on higher specification digital cameras. However, RAW is becoming more common in consumer digital cameras and RAW images can be downloaded into Elements in the same way as any other image. Once the RAW images are accessed, the Camera Raw dialog box opens so that a variety of editing functions can be applied to the image. RAW images act as a digital negative and have to be saved into another format before they can be used in the conventional way. To edit RAW images:

Don't forget

The RAW format should be used if you want to make manual changes to an image to achieve the highest possible quality.

Beware

RAW images are much larger in file size than the same versions captured as JPEGs.

Hot tip

All images can be opened in RAW by using the **File** > **Open in Camera Raw** command from the Menu bar.

1 Open a RAW image in the Editor or from the Organizer

2 In the Camera Raw dialog box, editing functions that are usually performed when an image is captured can be made manually

3 Click here to adjust the White Balance in the image

4 Drag these sliders to adjust the Color Temperature and Tint in the image

5 Drag these sliders to adjust the Exposure, Contrast, Highlights, Shadows, Whites and Blacks in the image

6 Click on the **Detail** tab and drag these sliders to adjust the Sharpness and Noise in the image

7 Click on the **Open Image** button. This opens the image in Expert edit mode, from where it can also be saved as a standard file format such as JPEG

The Sharpness of an image refers to the contrast between adjoining pixels, and can contribute to an image appearing more sharply in focus.

The Noise in an image refers to pixels that have not captured color accurately (mainly in low-level lighting) and can make images look "speckled". **Noise Reduction** in the RAW window can help reduce this, by dragging the available sliders.

Editing Multiple Images

The rise of digital cameras and smartphones with photographic capabilities means that we are now taking more photos than ever. In terms of editing, this can result in a lot of work if you want to perform similar or identical tasks on a number of images. However, in Elements there is an option for editing multiple files at the same time. This can be with a number of preset options, such as color quick fixes, renaming files and resizing files. To perform editing on multiple files:

The default file format for images taken with most digital cameras and smartphone cameras is JPEG (Joint Photographic Experts Group). However, this can be changed for a group of photos with the Process Multiple Files option.

1 In Expert edit mode, select **File** > **Process Multiple Files** from the Menu bar

2 The **Process Multiple Files** window contains all of the options for selecting and editing multiple files

Use the **Opened Files** option in Step 3 to perform a task on specific files, rather than on a whole folder.

3 Click here to select options for the source location of the images to be edited. This can be

either a folder, images imported from another location, or the currently-opened files

4 For the **Folder** option in Step 3, click on the **Browse...** button, navigate to the required folder and click on the **OK** button

Source:

Browse...

☐ Include All Subfolders
Destination:

☐ Same as Source

File Naming
☐ Rename Files

Document Name

Example: MyFile001.gif

Compatibility: ☑ Window

Image Size
☐ Resize Images

Width: Centim

Browse for Folder ✕

Choose a folder for processing multiple files...

∨ 🖭 Pictures
     📁 2013-07
     📁 2013-08
     📁 2013-09
     📁 2013-10
     📁 2013-12
     📁 2014-02
     📁 2014-03
     📁 2014-04
     📁 2014-05
     📁 2014-05-15

OK   Cancel

Beware

The more images in a folder, the longer it will take to process.

5 Select a destination folder in the same way as for selecting the source folder

Source:

C:\Users\Nick\Pictures\2014-05-15\   Browse...

☐ Include All Subfolders
Destination:

C:\Users\Nick\Pictures\Processed\   Browse...

☐ Same as Source

Beware

If you select the **Same as Source** option for the source of the processed files, these will overwrite the originals, even if the **Rename Files** option has been selected (it becomes deselected if Same as Source is selected).

6 Under the **Quick Fix** section, check on any of the fixes that you want applied to all of the images. The options are for **Auto Levels**, **Auto Contrast**, **Auto Color** and **Sharpen**

Quick Fix

☐ Auto Levels
☑ Auto Contrast
☑ Auto Color
☑ Sharpen

Hot tip

The Quick Fix options are a good way to edit a group of photos that have been taken under similar lighting conditions.

...cont'd

7 Under the **Image Size** section, check **On** the **Resize Images** checkbox and enter the required dimensions and resolution. If **Constrain Proportions** is checked **On**, only one of the Width or Height boxes has to be completed, as the other one will be adjusted automatically, in proportion

Beware

PDF and TIFF file formats generally produce larger file sizes than JPEGs, which is a file format specifically designed to compress file size.

8 Check **On** the **Convert Files to:** button to select an option for converting the files into another file format; e.g. as PDFs or TIFFs

Don't forget

Once all of the required selections have been made for converting the files, click on the **OK** button.

OK

9 Check **On** the **Rename Files** button to rename the batch of files based on a base document name and a sequential identifier

Applying Actions

Within Elements there are a number of preset editing actions that can be applied to images repeatedly, without having to perform all of the separate tasks individually. To do this:

1 In Expert edit mode, open the image to which you want to apply the action

2 Select **Window** > **Actions** from the Menu bar. Click here next to an Actions folder to expand it

3 Click on an action to select it

4 Click on this button to perform the action

5 The action is performed and all of the required editing steps are applied to the image

The Actions panel does not have a keyboard shortcut.

Beware

You cannot create your own actions within Elements.

Hot tip

If you have the full version of Photoshop, you can import Actions from there. To do this, click on the Actions panel's menu (top, right corner) and select **Load Actions**. Navigate to the Actions folder within the Photoshop program files (**Presets** > **Actions**) and select an action there. Click on the **Load** button to add it.

Managing Catalogs

Elements manages your photos in catalogs, in which all of your photos are organized. By default, this is done in a single catalog, known as My Catalog. This can contain all of your photos and you can search for them using keywords, tags or by album. However, once you have thousands of photos covering dozens of subjects, this can start to get a little overwhelming. One option is to create new catalogs that can be used for specific subjects; e.g. one for travel and one for business. To create and manage different catalogs:

Catalogs cannot be accessed from any of the Editor modes.

The existence of catalogs does not change the physical locations of photos; they still remain in their original folders.

172

When a catalog is selected in Step 2, there is also an option to repair it. This can be done if images have been moved or deleted since the catalog was created.

1 In the Organizer, select **File** > **Manage Catalogs...** from the Menu bar

2 The Catalog Manager dialog window displays the current catalog. Click here to select it and access options such as **Rename** or **Move**

3 Click on the **New...** button to create a new catalog

New...

4 Enter a name for the new catalog

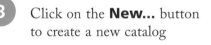

5 Click on the **OK** button

OK

6 Click on the **Start Importing** button to add photos to the new catalog

Start Importing

7 Check **On** the **Pictures** checkbox in the left-hand panel and click on individual folders in the main window to select or deselect them

8 Click on the **Import** button to add selected folders

9 The photos are imported into the new catalog

10 If keywords have been attached to any of the photos being imported, you will be able to include

the Keyword tags. Check **On** the checkboxes next to the required keywords and click on the **OK** button

11 The new catalog is created and displayed within the Catalog Manager dialog window

Hot tip

Blank catalogs can be created by clicking on the **Cancel** button in the **Import Media** window in Step 7. Media can then be added to the new catalog from a camera or memory card, or a folder, using the **Import** option.

Don't forget

Make the names of catalogs as appropriate as possible to the intended subject matter.

Don't forget

Photos can be added to more than one catalog.

173

12 The photos in the new catalog are displayed in the same way as for the default catalog

Viewing File Info

When digital images are taken, they create a considerable amount of related information, also known as metadata. To view this:

 Open an image in Expert or Quick edit mode

 Select **File** > **File Info** from the Menu bar

 Click on the **Camera Data** button to view the information (metadata) that was created when the image was captured

`Camera Data`

4 The Camera Data information includes the **Camera Information**; i.e. the make and model of the camera, and the **Shot Information**; i.e. Focal Length, Exposure, Image Size, Orientation, Resolution and Flash

Camera Information	
Make:	Canon
Model:	Canon EOS 350D DIGITAL; S/N: 2630703875
Owner:	
Lens:	

Shot Information	
Focal Length:	21.00 mm
Exposure:	1/30 sec; f/4.0; ISO 800; Aperture priority; Pattern metering
Image Size:	3456 x 2304
Orientation:	1 (Normal)
Resolution:	72.00 Pixel per Inch
Flash:	Did not fire

5 Click on the **Basic** button to add your own additional metadata to the image

`Basic`

Document Title:	
Author:	
	ⓘ Semicolons or commas can be used to separate multiple values
Author Title:	
Description:	
Rating:	☆ ☆ ☆ ☆ ☆
Description Writer:	
Keywords:	
	ⓘ Semicolons or commas can be used to separate multiple values
Copyright Status:	Unknown ▼
Copyright Notice:	
Copyright Info URL:	
Creation Date:	01/01/2018 11:26:02
Modification Date:	08/02/2018 13:44:27
Application:	Adobe Photoshop Elements 14.0 (Windows)

Don't forget

The **Shot Information** is created by the camera when a photo is taken.

Beware

Add a **Copyright Status** and a **Copyright Notice** in Step 5 if your photos are going to be published in public, and you are concerned that they may be used by others without your permission.

Save for Web

As digital cameras get more powerful in terms of the size and quality of images that they can capture, one issue is how to use these images on the web or in email: the larger the image, the longer it takes to send in an email or upload to the web. To overcome this, there is an option to save an image specifically for web use. To do this:

1. Open an image in Expert or Quick edit mode

2. Select **File > Save for Web** from the Menu bar to open the Save for Web window

3. The size of the original image is shown in the left-hand panel; the new size in the right-hand panel

4. Click here to select a file format for the image for the web

5. Enter a new size for the image to reduce the physical size of it; e.g. from 3024 x 3024 pixels to 500 x 500 pixels

6. The size of the image in the right-hand panel is reduced accordingly (in this example, to 208K)

Image Size

The physical size of a digital image can sometimes be a confusing issue, as it is frequently dealt with under the term "resolution". Unfortunately, resolution can be applied to a number of areas of digital imaging: image resolution, monitor resolution, print size and print resolution.

Image resolution

The resolution of an image is determined by the number of pixels it contains. This is counted as a vertical and a horizontal value; e.g. 4000 x 3000. When multiplied together it gives the overall resolution; i.e. 12,000,000 pixels in this case. This is frequently the headline figure quoted by camera manufacturers; e.g. 12 million pixels (or more commonly, 12 megapixels). To view the image resolution in Elements:

Hot tip

The keyboard shortcut for the Image Size dialog window is Alt + Ctrl + I (Alt + Command key + I on a Mac).

Hot tip

To view an image at its actual size, or the size at which it will currently be printed, select the **Zoom** tool from the Toolbox and select **1:1** or **Print Size** from the Tool Options bar.

176

Don't forget

The Resolution figure under the Document Size heading is used to determine the size at which the image will be printed. If this is set to 96 pixels/inch, then the onscreen size and the printed size should be roughly the same.

1 Select **Image > Resize > Image Size** from the Menu bar

2 The image size is displayed here (in pixels)

Image Size	
Learn more about: Image Size	OK / Cancel / Help

Pixel Dimensions: 34.9M

Width: 3027 pixels
Height: 4035 pixels

Document Size:
Width: 10.09 Inches
Height: 13.45 Inches
Resolution: 300 Pixels/Inch

☐ Scale Styles
☑ Constrain Proportions
☐ Resample Image:
Bicubic (best for smooth gradients)

Monitor resolution

Most modern computer monitors display digital images at between 72 and 96 pixels per inch (PPI). This means that every inch of the screen contains approximately this number of pixels. So, for an image being displayed at 100%, the onscreen size will be the number of pixels horizontally divided by 72 (or 96, depending on the monitor), and the same vertically. In the above example, this would mean the image, at actual size, could be viewed at approximately 31 inches by 42 inches (3027/96 and 4035/72) on a monitor. In modern web browsers, this is usually adjusted so that the whole image is accommodated on the viewable screen.

Document size (print resolution)

Pixels in an image are not a set size, which means that images can be printed in a variety of sizes, simply by contracting or expanding the available pixels. This is done by changing the resolution in the Document Size section of the Image Size dialog box. (When dealing with document size, think of this as the size of the printed document.) To set the size at which an image will be printed:

1 Select **Image** > **Resize** > **Image Size** from the Menu bar

2 Change the resolution here (or change the width and height of the document size). Make sure the Resample Image box is not checked (see page 178)

Image Size

Learn more about: Image Size   OK   Cancel   Help

Pixel Dimensions: 34.9M
Width: 3027 pixels
Height: 4035 pixels

Document Size:
Width: 20.18 Inches
Height: 26.9 Inches
Resolution: 150 Pixels/Inch

Scale Styles
Constrain Proportions
Resample Image:
Bicubic (best for smooth gradients)

3 By changing one value, the other two are updated too

Document Size:
Width: 15 Inches
Height: 19.995 Inches
Resolution: 201.8 Pixels/Inch

4 Click on the **OK** button   OK

Hot tip

To work out the size at which an image will be printed, divide the pixel dimensions (height and width) by the resolution value under the Document Size heading.

Don't forget

The print resolution determines how many pixels are used in each inch of the printed image (PPI). However, the number of dots used to represent each pixel on the paper is determined by the printer resolution, measured in dots per inch (DPI). So if the print resolution is 72 PPI and the printer resolution is 2880 DPI, each pixel will be represented by 40 colored dots; i.e. 2880 divided by 72.

177

Resampling Images

All digital images can be increased or decreased in size. This involves adding or removing pixels from the image. Decreasing the size of an image is relatively straightforward and involves removing redundant pixels. However, increasing the size of an image involves adding pixels by digital guesswork. To do this, Elements looks at the existing pixels and works out the nearest match for the ones that are to be added. Increasing or decreasing the size of a digital image is known as "resampling".

Resampling

Resampling down decreases the size of the image, and it is more effective than resampling up. To do this:

The process of adding pixels to an image to increase its size is known as "interpolation".

To keep the same resolution for an image, resample it by changing the Pixel Dimensions' height and width.
To keep the same Document Size (i.e. the size at which it will be printed) resample it by changing the resolution.

Make sure the Constrain Proportions box is checked On if you want the image to be increased or decreased in size proportionally.

1 Select **Image > Resize > Image Size** from the Menu bar

2 Check **On** the **Resample Image:** box

3 Resample the image by changing the pixel dimensions, the height and width, or the resolution

Image Size

Learn more about: Image Size

Pixel Dimensions: 15.3M

Width: 2000 Pixels

Height: 2666 Pixels

Document Size:

Width: 6.667 Inches

Height: 8.887 Inches

Resolution: 300 Pixels/Inch

☐ Scale Styles
☑ Constrain Proportions
☑ Resample Image:
Bicubic (best for smooth gradients)

OK   Cancel   Help

4 Changing any of the values in the Image Size dialog box alters the physical size of the image. Click on the **OK** button

Pixel Dimensions: 3.81M

Width: 1000 Pixels

Height: 1333 Pixels

11 Printing Images

This chapter details sizing images and printing them in a variety of formats.

Print Size

Before you start printing images in Elements, it is important to ensure that they are going to be produced at the required size. Since the pixels within an image are not a set size, the printed dimensions of an image can be altered according to your needs. This is done by specifying how many pixels are used within each inch of the image. The more pixels per inch (PPI), then the higher the quality of the printed image, but the smaller in size it will be.

To set the print size of an image (in any of the Editor modes):

The higher the resolution in the Document Size section of the dialog, the greater the quality, but the smaller the size of the printed image.

1 Open an image and select **Image** > **Resize** > **Image Size** from the Menu bar

2 Uncheck the **Resample Image:** box. This will ensure that the physical image size (i.e. the number of pixels in the image) remains unchanged when the resolution is changed

The output size for a printed image can be worked out by dividing the pixel dimensions (the width and height) by the resolution. So if the width is 2560, the height 1920, and the resolution 300 PPI, the printed image will be approximately 8 inches by 6 inches.

Image Size

Learn more about: Image Size

[OK]
[Cancel]
[Help]

Pixel Dimensions: 34.9M

Width: 3024 pixels
Height: 4032 pixels

Document Size:

Width: 51.21 Centimeters
Height: 68.28 Centimeters
Resolution: 150 Pixels/Inch

☐ Scale Styles
☑ Constrain Proportions
☐ Resample Image:

Bicubic (best for smooth gradients)

As long as the Resample Image box is unchecked, changing the output resolution has no effect on the actual number of pixels in an image.

3 The current resolution and document size (print size) are displayed here

4 Enter a new figure in the **Resolution:** box (here, the resolution has been increased from 150 to 300). This affects the document size; i.e. the size at which the image prints

Viewing print size
In Expert edit mode, images can be viewed at their print size:

1 Click on the Zoom tool

2 In the Tool Options, click on the **Print Size** button

3 The image is displayed at the size at which it will be printed. Change the resolution to see how this changes the print size

Hot tip

The keyboard shortcut for accessing the Image Size dialog window is Alt + Ctrl + I (Alt + Command key + I on a Mac).

Don't forget

A resolution of 300 pixels per inch (PPI) is a good benchmark for printed images. However, a lower resolution will still produce a good quality and enable the image to be printed at a larger size.

Beware

The print size on screen may not be completely accurate, depending on the resolution of your monitor. However, it will still give a reasonably good idea of the size of the printed image.

Print Functions

The Print functions in Elements can be accessed from the Menu bar in either the Editor or the Organizer, by selecting **File** > **Print**. Also, all of the print functions can be selected from Create mode. To print to your local printer using this method:

Hot tip

The keyboard shortcut for printing images is Ctrl + P, in either Editor or Organizer mode (Command key + P on a Mac).

Don't forget

The currently-active images are shown in the left-hand panel of the Print window.

Hot tip

Check **On** the **Crop to Fit** checkbox to crop the photo to ensure it fits on the page. Check the photo to ensure that it still appears as required.

1 Select an image in either the Editor or the Organizer, click on the **Create** button and click on the **Photo Prints** button

2 Click on the **Local Printer** button

3 The main print window displays the default options for how the printed image will appear, and also options for changing the properties of the print

4 Click the **Add...** button to include more images in the current print job, or select an image and click on the **Remove** button to exclude it

5 Use these options to rotate an image for printing, or change its size or position

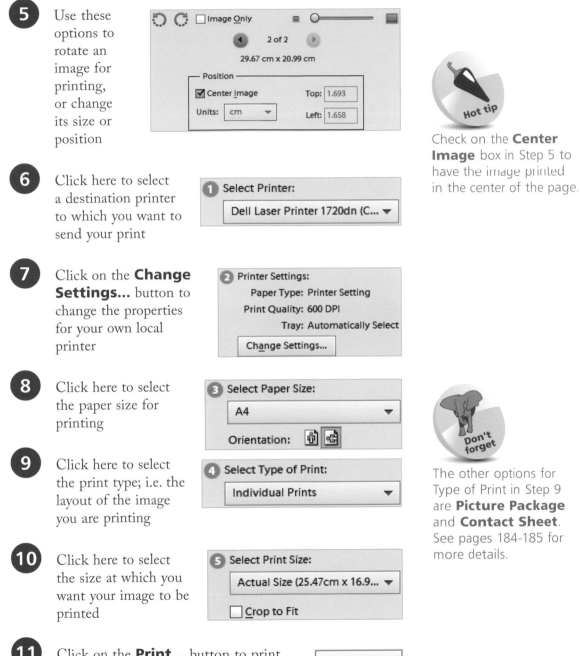

Check on the **Center Image** box in Step 5 to have the image printed in the center of the page.

6 Click here to select a destination printer to which you want to send your print

7 Click on the **Change Settings...** button to change the properties for your own local printer

8 Click here to select the paper size for printing

9 Click here to select the print type; i.e. the layout of the image you are printing

The other options for Type of Print in Step 9 are **Picture Package** and **Contact Sheet**. See pages 184-185 for more details.

10 Click here to select the size at which you want your image to be printed

11 Click on the **Print...** button to print your image with the settings selected above

183

Print Layouts

Rather than just offering the sole function of printing a single image on a sheet of paper, Elements has two options that can be used when printing images, which can help reduce the number of sheets of paper used.

Picture Package
This can be used to print out copies of different images on a single piece of paper. To do this:

Hot tip

When buying a printer, choose one that has borderless printing. This means that it can print to the very edge of the page.

Don't forget

The Picture Package option is also available if you print photos using **File** > **Print** (or Ctrl + P; Command + P on a Mac) from the Menu bar. In the **Prints** dialog window, select **Picture Package** under the **Select Type of Print:** heading.

Don't forget

The Picture Package function is useful for printing images in a combination of sizes, such as for family portraits.

 Select an image in either the Editor or the Organizer, click on the Create button, and then click on the **Picture Package** button

 The layout for the Picture Package is displayed in the main print window

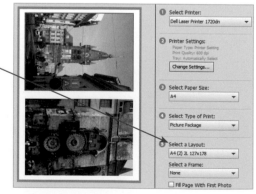

Under **Select a Layout:**, select how many images you want on a page and if required, select a type of frame for the printed images

184

Contact Sheet

This can be used to create and print thumbnail versions of a large number of images. To do this:

 Select an image in either the Editor or the Organizer, click on the Create button and then click on the **Contact Sheet** button

 The layout for the Contact Sheet is displayed in the main Print window

Don't forget

When a Contact Sheet is created, new thumbnail images are generated. The original images are unaffected.

Click under **Select Type of Print:** and select the number of columns to be displayed on the Contact Sheet

Beware

Do not include too many thumbnails on a Contact Sheet, otherwise they may be too small to see any detail clearly.

Creating PDF Files

PDF (Portable Document Format) is a file format that is used to maintain the original formatting and style of a document, so that it can be viewed on a variety of different devices and types of computers. In general, it is usually used for documents that contain text and images, such as information pamphlets, magazine features, and chapters from books. However, image files such as JPEGs can also be converted into PDFs, and this can be done within Elements without the need for any other specialist software. To do this:

PDF files are an excellent way to share files so that other people can print them. All that is required is a copy of Adobe Acrobat Reader, which is bundled with most software packages on computers, or can be downloaded from the Adobe website at **www.adobe.com**

1 Open an image and select **File** > **Save As** from the Menu bar

2 Select a destination folder and make sure the format is set to Photoshop PDF, then click **Save**

File name:	Prague2
Save as type:	Photoshop PDF (*.PDF;*.PDP)

Save Options

Organize: ☑ Include in the Elements Organizer
☑ Save in Version Set with Original

Save: ☐ As a Copy
☐ Layers
Color: ☑ ICC Profile: sRGB IEC61966-2.1
Other: ☐ Thumbnail

e Folders | Save

3 The PDF file is created and can be opened in Adobe Acrobat or Elements

PDF files are generally larger in terms of file size than standard image file formats such as JPEG.

Index